BOOKS IN THE DOCK

BOOKS IN THE DOCK

C. H. Rolph

ANDRE DEUTSCH

FIRST PUBLISHED 1969 BY
ANDRE DEUTSCH LIMITED
105 GREAT RUSSELL STREET
LONDON WC1
COPYRIGHT © 1969 BY C. H. ROLPH
ALL RIGHTS RESERVED
PRINTED IN GREAT BRITAIN BY
TONBRIDGE PRINTERS LTD
TONBRIDGE KENT

SBN 233 95901 7

CONTENTS

FOREWORD
by John Mortimer Q.C.

Writers should no doubt, if they ever stop to think of it, feel
complimented by the fact that so many people, in and out
of authority, regard all print with deep fear and suspicion.
Words are seen as unexploded mines, lying on deserted
beaches, which may be gingerly approached in the course of
morning walks, cautiously examined, perhaps prodded with
a stick; but ever likely to blow up in the faces of passers by,
destroying private property and changing the face of the
landscape for generations to come. The fear is natural; but
the average working writer is too modest to understand it.
Rarely does he stop to consider that the grubby, black
symbols with which he struggled among the cups of tea and
by the gas fire of his humble home can change lives and
alter societies. And when faced by lawyers and politicians
who, aware of his value, try to censor him, his attitude is
forever bewildered, and unexpectedly hurt.

To a writer the whole thing is perfectly simple. Life is
his subject. There can be no area of it forbidden to him.
The reader's participation and involvement is his aim:
horror and disgust are as obvious techniques in securing such
involvement as laughter and delight. In the *Last Exit* Appeal
a most intelligent and sympathetic Court heard these
literary clichés propounded as if for the first time, thought
them over and were inclined to agree. A fragile, perhaps
temporary bridge was then thrown over the great gulf that
exists between the artist and authority, on which that
gloomy but powerful work was able to scuttle to safety.

7

Mr. Rolph's first class study of the obscenity laws may provide a more permanent structure. Once we have all read it we shall know precisely where we are: even if all we discover is that we are moving in a deep legal fog, exchanging threats and insults across the great divide.

For an obscenity trial is in fact nothing less than a clash between two societies, both of which are adopting more or less false attitudes imposed by an illogical law. To the lawyers and judges, obscene literature must be something that 'depraves and corrupts' – but depraves and corrupts whom? Never them, of course, and not the jury. Not even the fourteen year old schoolgirl referred to in the *Philanderer* case – nowadays probably more sophisticated than any lawyer. But somewhere surely there must be some village Parsifal who is capable of being corrupted by a page of print. (In the *Last Exit* trial, Sir Basil Blackwell, an elderly Oxford bookseller of unsullied repute, volunteered for this unlikely role.) So the lawyers and politicians pretend, afraid to let the writers completely free, obscurely conscious that some unnamed principle of society is at stake: not quite realising that they are in far greater danger from Milton and Marx than they ever were from *Fanny Hill*.

The writer and expert legal witnesses have to pretend also. To pretend that good books are, in fact, for the Public Good, which is surely nonsense. Whoever was done good to by Stendhal or Baudelaire or Ronald Firbank? The virtue of much literature is that it is dangerous and may do you extreme harm. There also has to be a great pretence that much good writing is not deliberately and successfully erotic. The writer in an obscenity trial must keep it quite secret that he merely wants to express himself totally and quite rightly doesn't give a damn about the Public Good. So, under the smoke screen provided by Mr. Roy Jenkins's well intentioned and totally confusing piece of legislation known as the Obscene Publications Act 1959, the two sides advance stealthily to battle.

The truth of the matter is that a good book reveals the world of the person who wrote it. It may be a sick, dangerous and hallucinated world: and it is only important to enter it if you believe that all possible worlds should be entered.

Many people, including some jurors and many lawyers, do not share this belief. They prefer a safer, more limited form of existence. Such people will always find the condemnation of books perfectly natural: because the question they ask is 'Why do we need this writer's book?' and not 'Why did *he* need it?'

Mr. Rolph guides us easily and expertly through the legal maze, from the days when our present definition of obscenity was coined, days when one of the burning questions was 'What could be more obscene than the Venus in the Dulwich Art Gallery?', to our present period of puzzled concern. All right. We have got *Last Exit* and *Lady Chatterley* – But what lies ahead? We may have to defend de Sade, a writer of world wide significance most hard to place in the neat legal pigeon hole of Public Good. And yet a law which refused to allow the publication of de Sade would be a law which hamstrung the study of modern literature.

Mr. Rolph deals with the arguments for law reform: which lead to that almost unanswerable final query: what sort of Obscenity Law do we need, if any? 'Hard core' pornography is something everyone says they are against; but what exactly 'hard core' is seems impossible to define. And is a man really depraved if he masturbates with the help of some written fantasy – a practise which may well prevent him from acting out such fantasies in far more dangerous forms? The Danish experience has apparently been that the abolition of obscenity laws has led to a drop in the sale of erotic books; whereas the Victorian age, the great era of obscene prosecutions and *R. v. Hicklin*, might be described as the Golden Age of English Pornography. Logically, it may be thought, pornography, like prostitution, will always be more or less harmlessly with us: the only effect of the obscenity laws has been to give it a much needed air of mystery and excitement.

But, as Mr. Rolph conclusively proves, logic has never had the slightest effect on our approach to obscenity. Liberals who defend pornography would still like to ban books with fascist or racist arguments. The enlightened new Theatres Act, at last removing the Lord Chamberlain, condemns plays that tend to cause racial disharmony, which may be bad luck on *Othello* and the *Merchant of Venice*. Others wish to stop books dealing attractively with drug taking and violence. We all say that we are never frightened of words, provided we agree with them.

There's only one plea that I would make that may have escaped the almost infallible Mr. Rolph. I would like to form a society for the Defence of Bad Literature. Every writer has, it seems to me, the inalienable right to fail, and I think it's highly inequitable that the talented should be permitted access to erotic fields denied to the clumsy, talentless majority. We should not only be able to defend to the death other people's right to say things with which we disagree; we must also allow them to do it in abominable prose.

I

LAW
AND PUBLIC OPINION
TODAY

The Lawmaker's Dilemma

The discovery of obscenity can be compared with the fall of man, which it closely resembles. So far as censorship has to do with obscenity, censorship is the eternal figleaf. It is also today's demagogue, teacher, priest, psychiatrist, editor and commercial advertiser, exerting upon writer, printer and publisher a multitude of pressures. It is perhaps above all the law of defamatory libel. This book is concerned mainly with the swift modern development of what is called literary frankness and the lawmaker's dilemma in the face of it.

A growing number of people maintain that the lawmaker can solve his own dilemma, in this particular matter, by going out of business. At present he sustains a threefold apparatus of enforcement – the Director of Public Prosecutions (and for lesser jobs the police), the Customs and Excise Authorities, who seize 'indecent or obscene' books and other things when people try to import them, and the Post Office, which 'detects' such objects (or a hapless minority of them) when they are sent by post.

Censorship has become an epithet. Men apply it to the choices exercised by other men, usually when those other men are in a position of greater power and can impose their choices on the weaker. The central struggle can be seen to engage the revolt against paternalism, the 'devil's dance round authority', and the growing concern for privacy – now clearly threatened by new forces and techniques. It is in the literary world that this polarity finds its most articulate and intelligent expression, the advocates of 'total freedom' being, in the nature of things, more vehement as well as more eloquent than those who would retain some measure of control. But by way of illustrating, from the outset, the difficulty of saying what one wants in this complex matter, here are two statements reflecting the two points of view. First, a 'Resolution on Censorship' passed on the 5th May, 1968, at the annual general meeting of the National Council for Civil Liberties:

> This A.G.M. deplores prosecutions brought by the State, or by private individuals, with the intention of curbing freedom of artistic expression, which is essentially a matter of taste, and urges the Government to introduce legislation abolishing the offences of indecency, obscenity and blasphemy in all media of arts and communication.

It deplores prosecutions (the word itself leaves a loophole, which we will ignore) brought 'with the intention of curbing freedom of artistic expression'. Who would admit to such an intention? How could you prove it in a man? The intention is always to protect the young, the susceptible, those 'whose minds are open to immoral influences'; to protect, at any rate, someone else. If freedom of artistic expression is curbed in the process, well, the artist is not above the law and 'artistic' is a question-begging word. 'Which is essentially a matter of taste' – exactly: *de gustibus non disputandum.* 'Urges the Government to introduce legislation abolishing the offences of indecency. . . .' Yes? So that no publicly-vaunted depravity, however nauseating, is to be any concern of the law's? Is that the symbol of a secure and stable society?

Everyone knows what the National Council for Civil Liberties wants. For once that invaluable organisation, which would certainly have to be invented if it had not somehow happened, is expressing a minority view: books and pictures and the *avant garde* theatre count for little beside Association Football, the pools, bingo and the pub. But the Council is concerned with 'the things of the mind' no less than with the right to play soccer or bingo. Its protégés include the man buying his pools postal order, who would be quite likely to condemn Joyce and D. H. Lawrence as filthy swine, no less than scholarly dreamers like the late Sir Herbert Read, who wrote that 'in all the turbid chaos of modern literature Joyce and Lawrence are among the few authors who give us the conviction that the spirit of God is still manifest in the creative genius of man, still brooding on the face of the waters'.[1] Yet I hope I have shown that the National Council for Civil Liberties has succeeded no better than most of us do, by its Resolution on Censorship, in saying what it really wants.

Next, an extract from Lord Devlin's famous lecture on *The Enforcement of Morals*:[2]

> An established morality is as necessary as good government to the welfare of society. Societies disintegrate from within more frequently than they are broken up by external pressures. There is disintegration when no common morality is observed, and history shows that the loosening of moral bonds is often the first stage of disintegration, so that society is justified in taking the same steps to preserve its moral code as it does to preserve its government and other essential institutions.

And later Lord Devlin says this:

> I do not think one can ignore disgust if it is deeply felt and not manufactured. Its presence is a good indication that the bounds of toleration are being reached. Not everything is to be tolerated. No society can do without intolerance, indignation and disgust; they are the forces behind the moral law, and indeed it can be argued that if they or something like them are not present the feelings of society cannot be weighty enough to deprive the individual of freedom of choice.

It is not easy to isolate the subjectivity in Lord Devlin's luminous prose, but clearly enough 'the loosening of moral bonds' is being seen as a warning that national decline is on the way, 'the first stage of disintegration'.

Some of Lord Devlin's critics have thought that he was confusing cause and effect; that, in other words, the loosening of morals was more probably the consequence than the cause

1. *Does Pornography Matter?* Routledge, London, 1961.
2. Maccabean Lecture in Jurisprudence of the British Academy, 1959 (O.U.P.).

of a declining national prestige and influence in the world.
I doubt that the profoundest study of history and the collapse
of empires would enable one to say with confidence which had
ever come first, the moral decadence or the political ruin. If
in our day the British are 'morally decadent', it may be
because they are less important. It is easier to be virtuous
when you are busy. But I believe Lord Devlin to be right
when he says that no society can do without disgust and
indignation. It is this realisation, and the faulty language of
the law about obscenity, that have to be taken into account
by the lawyer who is asked to advise whether it would be
'safe' to publish a book. This falls to the lot of many a
practising solicitor, and for no very clear reason it is usually a
solicitor experienced in defamatory libel – perhaps because
publishers get to know such solicitors and because they, in
turn, get to know juries. Let us pretend, for a moment, to be
such a solicitor asked to advise upon a manuscript.

The 1959 Act

As the law stands, the will of the people and the task of the
jury are supposed to be reflected in Section I of the Obscene
Publications Act 1959, which sets out to punish anyone who
publishes an obscene article, whether for gain or not. Each of
those three words – publishes, obscene and article – repre-
sents a long legislative pregnancy. Here is what they now
mean:

Publishes:
(a) 'distributes, circulates, sells, lets on hire, gives or lends,
    or offers for sale or for letting on hire; or

(b) 'in the case of an article containing or embodying
    matter to be looked at, or a record, shows, plays or
    projects it.' (This doesn't apply to television, sound
    broadcasting or public cinemas, all of which are
    otherwise controlled; but it *does* seem to apply, at the
    end of a bewildering course of mutually cancelling
    phrases and double negatives, to a film shown in a
    private dwelling house, whether or not you have to
    pay to see the show.)

Obscene:

An article is obscene 'if its effect or (where the article comprises two or more distinct items) the effect of any one of its items is, if taken as a whole, such as to tend to deprave and corrupt persons who are likely, having regard to all relevant circumstances, to read, see or hear the matter contained or embodied in it.'

Article:

'Any description of article containing or embodying matter to be read or looked at or both, any sound record, and any film or other record of a picture or pictures.'

Publication

Come back now to the word 'publishes'. The phrase 'sells, lets on hire, gives or lends' means publication to an individual, but 'distributes, circulates' involves more than one recipient. A mere 'offer for sale or letting for hire' is publishing. But simply putting a book in a shop window or on a display counter may be no more than what the law calls 'an invitation to treat' (i.e., how much is this worth to you?). As soon as this flaw was discovered, through the failure of a prosecution,[1] there began an agitation to get the Act changed and strengthened, in which a prominent part was played by a specially convened group of churchmen called the 'London Committee Against Obscenity'. (This had come into being at the instance of a number of youth organisations which sought the churches' protection – where, they said, the police had failed – against a flood of 'bulk pornography' coming in from the United States.) In 1964 Parliament approved an amending Act which created a new offence of *'having* an obscene article for publication for gain, whether gain to himself or gain to another'; after which it mattered no longer that the display in the window or on the counter might not be an 'offer for sale'; and it was possible, where it had not been before, to deal with wholesalers as distinct from booksellers and newsagents. But possessing an 'obscene article' for gain does *not* mean possessing a book you haven't read

1. *Mella* v. *Monahan* (1961), *Criminal Law Review,* p. 175.

and don't know to be obscene (whether you want to make any gain out of it or not); and as an accompaniment to this provision, there appeared in the 1964 Act the following extraordinary paragraph, which may be said to resemble the camel in that it has every characteristic of something designed by a committee:

> The question whether the article is obscene shall be determined by reference to such publication for gain of the article as in the circumstances it may reasonably be inferred he had in contemplation and to any further publication that could reasonably be expected to follow from it, but not to any other publication.

It only means that the jury has to consider who was likely to get hold of it *and* what kind of people he was likely to pass it on to. It rather took its pattern from a similar clause[1] in the 1959 Act, which is even more difficult, convoluted and camel-like:

> The question whether an article is obscene shall be determined without regard to *any publication by another person* unless it could reasonably have been expected that the publication by the other person would follow from publication by the person charged.

What does 'publication' mean here? It means, as always in this context and any legal context, the act of 'publishing' or showing. It doesn't mean a book, magazine, newspaper article, pamphlet. The clause means (I think) that a jury cannot, in deciding whether a book is obscene, consider whether anyone other than the defendant sold, gave or showed it to somebody – unless it is obvious that that was his purpose in getting it from the defendant. In 1960 in the Lady Chatterley case, even Mr. Justice Byrne seems to have misunderstood this. Mr. Gerald Gardiner, Q.C. (as he then was), defending Penguin Books Ltd., had been referring to an expurgated *Lady Chatterley's Lover* which, precisely because of its expurgations, was 'far more obscene than the book which is the subject-matter of this prosecution'. Mr. Mervyn Griffith-Jones, Q.C., for the Crown, rightly objected that

1. It is Section 2 (6).

'reference to other books now by way of comparison as to whether or not this is obscene is not allowed'. Whereupon the Judge (it seems to me mistakenly) quoted the above passage from Section 2 (6) as 'a Section in the Statute which deals with it':

> The question whether an article is obscene shall be determined without regard to any publication by another person unless it could reasonably have been expected that the publication by the other person would follow from publication by the person charged.

'Before the 1959 Act, of course,' said the Judge, 'the law was that you could not have a comparison of other books with the book charged, and the Statute now specifically allows that.'

It doesn't, but the point was allowed to pass, Mr. Gerald Gardiner saying no more than: 'My Lord, in my submission that sub-section is dealing with quite another matter.' The episode serves to illustrate how one of the astutest of Judges (he had been Senior Treasury Counsel at the Old Bailey, in which capacity he had advised the Director of Public Prosecutions about many an 'obscene' book) could be misled by the Act of Parliament on which a publisher's legal adviser must now base the opinion he is so often asked to give.

Now consider paragraph (b) under the word 'publishes' on page 14. What's 'an article containing or embodying matter to be looked at'? It is a film or a model, a picture or sculpture, or something similarly tangible which, if it happens to be 'obscene', the law prefers you not to look at. And because this might not have included a gramophone or tape recording, the legislators added 'or a record'. But it still wasn't careful enough. In 1963[1] the High Court had to agree that it had not included photographic negatives seized by the police, since these can be neither 'shown, played nor projected'. So Parliament took the opportunity offered by the 1964 Act to bring in:

> anything which is intended to be used, either alone or as one of a set, for the reproduction or manufacture therefrom of articles . . .

1. *Straker* v. *D.P.P.*, 1 Q.B. 926, D.C.

The Meaning of 'Obscene'

We pass on to the word 'obscene' (look at page 15). A book or story is obscene if its effect, *taken as a whole*, is such as to tend to deprave and corrupt persons who are likely . . . to read it. It does not need to deprave or corrupt anyone. It is not necessary that anyone thus susceptible should have read it. Its 'effect' is not, therefore, its effect upon any person. Its effect is its completion, the result of bringing together its component parts. It is something very close to its author's *intention*, the factor that has sustained the greatest argument throughout the recent history of the obscenity laws and their enforcement. And yet it will be judged on a mere 'tendency' – does it tend to deprave and corrupt?

To tend is 'to have a specified result if allowed to act: to lead or conduce to some state or condition'.[1] To deprave is (in the current sense) 'to make morally bad'.[2] To corrupt is 'to render morally unsound; to pervert (a good quality); to debase, defile.'[3] Our Judaeo-Christian inheritance of 'sin' has ensured that 'morally bad' and 'morally unsound' mean sexually promiscuous or licentious; and to deprave or corrupt someone may accordingly be to make him think how nice it would be to become sexually promiscuous or licentious. To debase or defile, on the other hand, may be merely to coarsen or pollute a mind hitherto given to higher things.

This is as near, I think, as words can get to the meaning of this oft-used phrase.

During the prosecution of Calder & Boyars Ltd for publishing (in 1966) the American novel *Last Exit to Brooklyn*, Sir Basil Blackwell was called as an expert witness for the Crown, to rebut defence experts as to the book's literary and artistic merit. Sir Basil, a cultivated and widely-read man of 79, and a Magistrate himself, told the Marlborough Street Magistrate that 'the interests of literature would be little impaired' if the book were forgotten. 'It is a vile book,' he said, 'written, I think, with some relish.' And then in cross-examination he was asked whether anyone could be depraved or corrupted by it?

1, 2 and 3. *Shorter Oxford Dictionary.*

'It depraved and corrupted me to some extent', Sir Basil declared. 'I define "to deprave and corrupt" as "to impair, spoil, debase, defile". I am afraid my memory, in the few years that remain to me, will not be purged of it.'

He had taken the trouble, he said later at a London meeting,[1] to acquaint himself, before going to Court, with the OED definitions of these words. He implicitly disclaimed that at 79 a man can be induced by a book to contemplate a life of sexual promiscuity or licentiousness; but he impressively supported a growing theory that a balanced mind, as an instrument of social value, can be impaired and polluted by disgust. Yet juries are commonly told that a capacity to feel disgust – the quality which Lord Devlin regards as essential to society[2]– is not what they are concerned with. This is how Lord Gardiner put it to the jury in his defence of *Lady Chatterley's Lover*:

The words deprave and corrupt mean in ordinary life, do they not, 'effect a change of character for the worse'? That is really what it comes to. There are various things which it does *not* mean, and various things which it is not your function to consider. It is *not* a question of whether you think the book is shocking. *It is not a question of whether you think the book is disgusting* or whether it is in good taste.

And in *R. v. Secker & Warburg* 1956, Mr. Justice Stable had said to his jury:

Remember the charge is a charge that the tendency of the book is to corrupt and deprave. The charge is not that the tendency of the book is to shock or disgust. That is not a criminal offence.

What is an 'Article'?

And, finally (we are still considering the words of the Obscene Publications Act 1959) there is the word 'article'. It was an unfortunate word to use in such a Statute, for it is so com-

1. At the National Book League, organised by the Society of Young Publishers, on the 30th May, 1968.
2. P. 13.

monly taken to mean a short essay or contribution to a
periodical. Let us look at the definition again:

> Any description of article containing or embodying matter
> to be read or looked at, or both, any sound record, and
> any film or other record of a picture or pictures.

To which, as we have seen, there was added in 1964 a phrase
specially designed to bring in photographic negatives. The
words 'read or looked at or both', coupled with the words
'read, see or hear' in the meaning of obscenity, caused the
utmost alarm among writers when they first appeared as a
Government amendment to Mr. Roy Jenkins's 1959 Bill.
Radio and television plays and sketches seemed suddenly
vulnerable. They might, until then, have thought themselves
immune from censorship, lulled into a false sense of security
by the vagueness and long quiescence of the Common Law.
But the proposed words did no more than give statutory
form to what the Common Law had always said (or had
always, in the bosoms of the Judges, been waiting to say
when it got out). The Home Office view was that if Mr.
Jenkins and his supporters wanted to abolish the Common
Law merely in relation to literature, then the Government
must do something to retain its control over other forms of
publicity and entertainment. What happened in fact was
that, by an adroit piece of Home Office sleight of hand, the
Common Law was preserved with only slight mutilation, for
use against literature hardly less than against other forms of
'obscenity'.

The Alternatives

All these things a lawyer would consider as he read any
manuscript put before him by his publisher client. He would
have much in mind the growing gravity of the penalties
that could follow conviction, and he would weigh the
chances of a criminal prosecution as against a move merely to
have the published book destroyed. If there were a successful
prosecution ending in the Magistrates' Court, there could be
a prison sentence of six months or a fine of £100. These,
today, are wildly disproportionate and suggest that the

Government (who insisted on them) saw the most likely offender as a man in a cloth cap to whom prison was a second home and £100 a small fortune. The six months' prison maximum confers a right of trial by jury (as does anything over three). And on conviction by a jury the maximum penalties are of mediaeval severity, namely three years' imprisonment plus a fine of unspecified amount – a fine without limit. The Bill's promoters were very shocked at this indication of severity from a Government that had been unexpectedly co-operative about the Bill, but they succumbed to the explanation (a) that it would be unconstitutional to tie the hands of Assize Court Judges in the matter of maximum fines and (b) that if you *did* fix a maximum, say £1,000, some Judges might think that was the proper sort of fine in all cases. Nobody *had* said £1,000, and it was known that there *were* cases in which the Judges' hands were tied in the matter of maximum fines, whether it was constitutional to tie them or leave them free. Among these cases were dangerous drugs offences, bribery, brothel-keeping, forgery of passports, and frauds by moneylenders. Indeed, the House of Commons Select Committee set up in 1957 to consider the Bill had themselves recommended a fine of £2,000; and there were some distinguished lawyers on that Committee.

But the penalties had to be accepted as the price of essential government support. In the event, the Courts have so far been fairly moderate, though they have tended to take it out in 'costs' (to which I will return).

The alternative – a 'destruction order' application – raises no essentially different problems, apart from the crucial distinction that it exposes to no other penalty than the burning of the books. It takes the form of a summons from a Magistrate, reciting (in effect) that some allegedly obscene books have been found and seized in a bookshop in his area and that he proposes to burn them unless the bookseller, the author or the publisher can 'show cause' why he shouldn't. Despite all the efforts of the Bill's promoters to have the Director of Public Prosecutions made responsible, until the *Last Exit to Brooklyn* case this machinery could be set in motion by any private citizen; and in that case it was Sir Cyril Black, M.P., who played the role of private citizen.

(Of which, more later.) Then in 1967 Mr. Roy Jenkins, as Home Secretary, made this powerful little addition to the Criminal Justice Bill, wherein it could hardly be said to belong (Mr. Quintin Hogg, his opposite number, emphatically pointed out that it did not):

> A justice of the peace shall not issue a warrant under Section 3 (1) of the Obscene Publications Act 1959 (search for and seizure of obscene articles) except on an information laid by or on behalf of the Director of Public Prosecutions or by a Constable.

It was the end of the Cyril Black kind of case. It did not, as many people unaccountably imagined (and stated in the public prints) at last confer the 'right of trial by jury' in these destruction order cases. It merely meant that if a book with any literary pretensions (or supposed by the DPP to have any) was to be tested in the Courts, it was now far more likely to be by prosecution than by destruction order proceedings. And, as the result of a prolonged battle during the Bill's passage through Committee, expert evidence as to the book's literary merit had already been made admissible in such proceedings exactly as in a criminal trial.

No 'Stale' Prosecutions?

How long is a book to run the gauntlet before its publisher can breathe freely and order that bigger second print? The DPP always used to have his favourite targets, and you saw them advertised (even if he didn't) as 'rare books' or 'collectors' books' in the weekly papers. Richard Carlile's *Every Woman's Book*, which today could well be a fourth-form needlework prize; *The Decameron*, that mausoleum of defeated pruriency; *The Well of Loneliness* (why, in God's name?); *The Sexual Impulse, Sleeveless Errand, Ulysses,* and so on to *Chatterley* and the modern belief that, if you choose your moment, you can publish anything. When The Bodley Head published *Ulysses* in 1937 they had the foresight, knowing that juries were being told (as they had been told for many years) to read a book 'as a whole', to print as an appendix the famous 1933 judgment of Judge Woolsey that ended with the words:

Ulysses is a sincere and honest book and I think that the criticisms of it are entirely disposed of by its rationale ... My considered opinion, after long reflection, is that whilst in many places the effect of *Ulysses* on the reader undoubtedly is somewhat emetic, nowhere does it tend to be an aphrodisiac. *Ulysses* may *therefore* be admitted into the United States.

Any prosecution of the Bodley Head *Ulysses* would thus have had to begin by requiring the jury to read its Woolsey vindication. It is tempting here to consider the implications, for Great Britain as well as for America, of the word 'therefore' italicised above. Admitted because it is nowhere an aphrodisiac? So an aphrodisiac would be kept out? Who would say that *Last Exit to Brooklyn* was an aphrodisiac? And so on. ... The temptation must be spurned.

But The Bodley Head waited many years before they could be sure that there would be no prosecution. Can they be sure now? Yes, so far as concerns their 1937 edition. If they bring out another in 1968 or 1969 they will be safe enough, for everyone knows what it says, no-one seems corrupted, and a successful film of it has been made. 'Our local cinema', wrote Mr. E. S. Turner in *Punch* (19th June, 1968), 'which must have screened *Snow White* and *Bambi* more often than any six cinemas put together, screwed up its courage and booked *Ulysses*. It screwed up its prices too.... Normally it's something you only learn about on walls.' And on the walls it was free, but not so well done. But fashions change and the Judges, no less than juries, sometimes form and sometimes follow public opinion. So there is a crumb of comfort in this brief provision in the Act of 1959 – it is Section 2 (3):

A prosecution on indictment for an offence against this section (i.e., publishing an 'obscene article') shall not be commenced more than two years after the commission of the offence.

Usually, for 'a prosecution on indictment' – a prosecution, that is to say, before a judge and jury – there is no limitation of time: you can be hauled into Court after a lifetime. What about prosecution or other proceedings before a Magistrate?

The limitation there is usually six months, but in this case it has been set at 12 months – the artful Home Office view being that this might benefit an author or publisher if six months *had* elapsed since publication; for in that event a six months' limit would leave the Crown with no option but to prosecute for the indictable offence and the heavier penalties!

But some of the joy goes out of this when you recall the meaning of 'publish'. Distribute, circulate, sell, let on hire, give, or lend. . . . The act of publishing, as we know it in the normal practice of publishing, is but one of all these alternatives. The crumb of comfort is a little the larger for Section 25 of the Criminal Justice Act 1967[1] – the DPP will not have, in practice, the decision in almost all cases whether to take action or not.

'Read it "As a Whole"'

When the 1959 Act finally emerged saying that the 'test of obscenity' must necessarily involve reading the book (or judging the 'article') *as a whole*, this was hailed as a victory for reform. But in fact it had been the *practice* of the law for almost a century. 'Read it as a whole, members of the jury,' said Mr. Justice Stable to his jury in *The Philanderer* case.[2] And in fact his careful summing up, resulting in the famous acquittal, did no more than restate the law as it had stood for a century. 'Newspapers from *The Times* to the *Church of England Newspaper*,' wrote Norman St. John Stevas in his *Obscenity and the Law*[3]

> published approving leading articles, but few of the leader writers noticed that the judge had left the law as formulated in the *Hicklin* case practically unchanged.

I was present at each of the 'big four' Old Bailey trials in 1956 – Hutchinson for publishing *September in Quinze* (convicted), Heinemann for *The Image and the Search* (acquitted), Arthur Barker for *The Man in Control* (acquitted), and Secker and Warburg for *The Philanderer* (acquitted). In all

1. See p. 22.
2. *R. v. Secker & Warburg*, 1956.
3. Secker & Warburg, London, 1956.

those cases the Judge (a different Judge for each) told the jury to 'read this book *as a whole*'; objections were raised in all of them when prosecuting counsel wanted to supply the jury with page numbers, so that they would know, as they read, when to be on the alert for the purple passages. But here is a story from the *Manchester Guardian* of 8th February, 1955, that illustrates both the difficulty of the reading programme and the temptation *not* to read a book as a whole:

Six Months to read Books

Summons Adjourned

After a member of the bench had protested about the time it would take to read the books, Smethwick (Staffordshire) magistrates yesterday adjourned the hearing of an obscene books summons until August 22.

The proprietor of a bookshop in Smethwick was summoned to show cause why 277 books seized at his shop should not be destroyed as obscene. The books, which represented 104 different publications, were handed to the magistrates and one of them, Mr. John Fallon, said: 'In these days when some magistrates are heavily engaged in businesses and professions, to have to read enormous numbers of these books – if it is going to be done at all conscientiously – is a time-absorbing process. I think some consideration should be given to this fact.'

The clerk (Mr. T. Craddock), said it was not necessary to read the whole of any particular book. 'If you come to a line which you think is sufficient to make the book obscene, that is enough.'

Mr Fallon: 'But that line may be saved until the last paragraph.'

The Expert Witnesses

Wherever 'that line' occurred, it could hardly be enough today, any more than it could then, to make a book obscene. Even if it could, even when a book has been adjudged obscene, its publication can as the law now stands be held to be for the public good:

A person shall not be convicted (says Section 4 (1) of the Obscene Publications Act 1959) of an offence against

Section 2 of this Act (publishing an obscene article) and an order for forfeiture shall not be made under Section 3 (having an obscene book for gain) if it is proved that publication of the article in question is justified as being for the public good on the ground that it is in the interests of science, literature, art or learning, or of other objects of general concern.

Parliament accepted this paradoxical proposal with surprisingly little enquiry. Possibly the law as it stood was felt to be so absurd in relation to works of literary imagination that almost anything could but be an improvement. What it means is that every trial involving a defence of literary merit proceeds (or this is the theory) by two stages. First the jury (or the magistrate) decides whether the book is obscene; and then proceeds to the decision whether it is, nevertheless, of such a literary or artistic or scientific standard that its obscenity is redeemed. But what that means, in turn, is that a book whose 'effect' is such that it 'tends to deprave and corrupt' those likely to read it is a book that can be for the public good. How depravity and corruption can be turned to the public good, merely because they are skilfully, artistically, or scientifically achieved, is a question that everyone turned away from until the Court of Appeal's decision in *Last Exit to Brooklyn* (see page 112). I hope to show that, if book censorship in this or any form is to stay with us, this procedure should take a more logical and face-saving form; but meanwhile this is how the same Section of the 1959 Act (in Sub-section 2) allows it to be done. The idea was by no means new:

(2) It is hereby declared that the opinion of experts as to the literary, artistic, scientific or other merits of an article may be admitted in any proceedings under this Act either to establish or to negative the said ground (i.e., the ground that publication is 'justified' in the interests of science, literature, etc.).

Sir James FitzJames Stephen, in his *Digest of the Criminal Law*, written in 1877, appends this 'submission' to his Article 228 – and subsequent Editors of his work have made no pretence that it is anything more than a submission, though Stephen wrote with immense authority as Judge, legal historian, and principal draftsman of the Criminal Law Consolidation Acts of 1861:

> A person is justified in exhibiting disgusting objects, or publishing obscene books, papers, writing, prints, pictures, drawings, or other representations, if their exhibition or representation is for the public good, as being necessary or advantageous to religion or morality, to the administration of justice, the pursuit of science, literature or art, or other objects of general interest; but the justification ceases if the publication is made in such a manner, to such an extent, or under such circumstances, as to exceed what the public good requires in regard to the particular matter published.

In a footnote to Article 228, Stephen remarks that 'the publication of an edition of Juvenal, Aristophanes, Swift, Defoe, Bayle's Dictionary, Rabelais, Brantôme, Boccaccio, Chaucer, etc., cannot be regarded as a crime: yet each of these books contains more or less obscenity for which it is impossible to offer any excuse whatever. I know not how the publication of them could be justified except by the consideration that upon the whole it is for the public good that the works of remarkable men should be published as they are, so that we may be able to form as complete an estimate as possible of their characters and of the times in which they lived' (this was a point strongly relied upon by Mr. Justice Stable in the *Philanderer* case). 'On the other hand' (continues Stephen's note), 'a collection of indecencies might be formed from any one of the authors I have mentioned, the separate publication of which would deserve severe punishment.'

And with some of those great names in mind, let us look back in literary history for the beginnings of this urge that some men have always felt to decide what other men should be allowed to read.

THE ORIGINS
OF CENSORSHIP

The Printing Press

When, in Chapter I, I compared the discovery of obscenity
with the fall of man, I was dabbling in first causes. Those who
believe it to be evil to make men think about their gender
have always seemed to suppose that their protégés thought
about it more when it became possible for them to read
about it. If they are right, the originator of depravity and
corruption on the modern scale is the man who invented
block printing; and you can take your choice between
Johann Gutenberg, who set up his press at Strasbourg in
1428, and Laurens Janszoen (who is sometimes called
Laurens Janszoen Koster, though Koster simply means that
he was a sexton or churchwarden). Janszoen is said to have
set up his press at Haarlem in the Netherlands 20 years
before Gutenberg's, and his supporters allege that a dishonest workman stole some of his apparatus, took it to
Strasbourg, set up first on his own and then took Gutenberg
into partnership. Whichever of them started it all, he bears
an awful responsibility and he has laid the foundation of
many fortunes.

Earlier readers, that is to say those of the Roman, Greek
and earlier civilisations, were perhaps corrupt already,
though the evil that could be done by Aristophanes, Plautus,
Terence, Juvenal and the rest who wrote all those obscene
plays and stories was confined to the privileged few who
could have them copied out or (not being slaves) could
gather round to hear them read or recited. Even so, Plato in
his *Republic* cites Socrates as being anxious that some bits

should be withheld from the young. Learned men still seem divided on the question whether this anxiety was concerned with 'love' or with depravity, no less than on the question whether pornography is intended to be, or can be, aphrodisiac. Here are two recent views: first the late Professor C. S. Lewis in the 1961 summer issue of the *Critical Quarterly*, writing about Ovid's use of what we call four-letter words:

> In a genuinely pornographic passage, by which I mean one *clearly intended to act as an aphrodisiac on the reader*,[1] Ovid has occasion to mention the thing; but he knows his trade far too well to use the word.

And Sir Alan Herbert, giving evidence on behalf of the Society of Authors to the House of Commons Select Committee on the Obscene Publications Bill[2]:

> We do say that the dominant effect is the thing that matters. You may get a phrase which may shock some old lady and may surprise some young girl, but *unless the whole purpose of the thing is, as I have said, to make people randy*,[3] or the author goes so far that it is against common decency, then we say that man ought to be left alone.

I don't believe that, in retrospect, Sir Alan would wish to do other than 'leave alone' an author whose purpose was aphrodisiacal; for the least of authors expects to produce *some* effect on his readers and would be depressed if he knew his erotic passages to be read as if they were railway time-tables. (Even those occasionally make the experienced traveller laugh.)

It was not until 1477, fifty years after Gutenberg began in Strasbourg, that William Caxton produced the first of his books in England, *The Sayings of the Philosophers* (Lord Rivers's version); but Caxton then proceeded to bring the existing literary masterpieces within the reach of that tiny minority of his countrymen who could read. He gave them Malory's *Morte d'Arthur* (attacked by literary critics a century later for its 'bold bawdry') and Chaucer's *Canterbury Tales*, fixing the English language for the first time after six centuries of rather chaotic development – and publishing the first of our printed

1 and 3. Italics mine.
2. *House of Commons Paper* No. 122 of 1958, p. 111, Q. 765.

'obscenities'. There was no daring in these two books; obscenity had not really been discovered and there was nothing to hush up. Until that time there had been no written bawdry outside the Church, which rather went in for it. Its earliest known priestly example seems to have been the *Codex Exoniensis*, a collection of poems and riddles presented to Exeter Cathedral by Bishop Leofric just before the Norman Conquest. The 'Exeter Book', as we now call it, would stand a slim chance with the jury that condemned *Last Exit to Brooklyn* in 1967, if they were given an honest translation.

The Licensing of Newspapers and Books

A century after the Caxton Press began operations the Stationers' Company, a City of London Livery, was incorporated by royal charter 'for the protection of manufacturers and readers of books'; and thenceforth – from 1557 – no one was allowed to set up a printing press without its permission. The 'protection' of selected booksellers and publishers turned out to mean the harassment of a much greater number not deemed worthy of protection, the Stationers' Company becoming (almost as a condition of the charter) an instrument of government censorship policy. The Wardens of the Company were actually empowered to arrest anyone obstructing them when they went to search a house or shop. They could burn the books they seized and they could send the obstructive inmate to prison for three months.

But not for obscenity. The government cared, still, only about sedition and religious heresy; and many a master printer was put to death for unlicensed publishing, when his theme was such that people might have been deflected to the wrong church on a Sunday. By 1586 Archbishop Whitgift was wielding censorship powers vested in him by the Star Chamber. No printing was allowed outside London, Oxford and Cambridge (the Eternal Loxbridge Triangle, as Logan Pearsall Smith called it). And in 1599 a translation of Ovid's *Elegies* by Christopher Marlow was burned at Stationers' Hall by order of the Archbishop – and this, at last, *was* on grounds of obscenity. The sixteenth century, at its very close, was watching the birth-pangs of 'literary merit', the expert witness, and the 'redemption by genius' that allowed the Shakespeare texts to come down to us more or less intact. And William Lambarde had appeared on the scene.

Lambarde drafted what was, in effect, the first 'Obscene Publications Bill'. He was a wealthy London jurist and antiquary, a bencher of Lincoln's Inn, and the founder of a famous hospital for the poor at Greenwich. In 1568 he had published an invaluable translation of the Saxon laws, and in 1576 the first 'County history' ever produced in England, *A Perambulation of Kent*. As a Kent Magistrate he published in 1581 a magistrates' manual called *Eirenarcha*, to which all subsequent writers in the same field have acknowledged their debt. And it was he who in 1580 promulgated a draft 'Act of Parliament for the Establishment of the Governors of the English Print'. Its 'long title' began as follows:

An Act to restrain the licentious printing, selling and uttering of unprofitable and hurtful English books . . .

And its preamble contained this masterly passage:

For the better control of poesies, sundry books, pamphlets, ditties, songs and other works and writings of many sorts and names serving (for a great part of them) to none other end (what titles soever they bear) but only to let in the main sea of wickedness and to set up an art of making lascivious ungodly love, to the high displeasure of God, whose gifts and graces be pitifully misused thereby, to the manifest injury and offence of the godly-learned, whose praiseworthy endeavours and writings are therefore the less read and regarded, to the intolerable corruption of common life and manners, which pestilently invades the minds of many that delight to hear or read the said wanton works, and to no small or sufferable waste of the treasure of this realm which is thereby consumed and spent in paper, being of itself a foreign and chargeable commodity . . .

The Bill was never in fact presented to Parliament, but it expresses (and preserves for our amusement) the mounting uneasiness of the clerics at the rapid spread of non-devotional reading. The opening reference to 'unprofitable and hurtful English books' probably meant that they were without profit to the minds of men, but there is evidence that more mundane profits were seen to be at risk, since people of a non-scholarly turn of mind were beginning to read for pleasure, and there was no knowing where that road could end. If, without anyone breathing down your neck, you were offered the choice of reading about virtue or reading about vice, you read about vice.

But in this Bill, behind the mixture of literary, moral, ecclesiastical and frankly financial anxiety may be seen the modern publishers' Garden of Eden. The preamble contains every argument and every cliché that is used in the censor-ship controversy today, from 'letting in the main sea of wickedness' and 'setting up an art of making ungodly love' to the 'intolerable corruption of common life and manners' among those wretched new literates who 'delight to read the said wanton works'. William Lambarde, it seems to me, stood at the crossroads in the history of English literature, pointing vainly in the direction he wanted us all to take and using in this context, for the first time, the explosive word 'corruption'. We went along the road marked Corruption, 'to the manifest injury and offence of the godly-learned'. But to the considerable material profit of many succeeding generations of profane publishers and writers. Licensing had fallen into disuse, mainly because the evasions were now so numerous that the law was inoperable. The consequent free-for-all lasted nearly a century.

The Responsibility of Cromwell and the Puritans

By the time the Stuarts had been overthrown and England had a Lord Protector, reading about sex had firmly acquired the character of a sin. It was now a positive evil, not a negative one exposed by any deflection of the reader from God. The 'act of love' had got on to paper, its ecstasy was now communicable, and to quite the wrong people. 'Are you telling me', Marie Antoinette is said to have asked her lover of the moment, 'that the poor do this kind of thing?' He said he thought it was quite frequent among them. 'Ridiculous!'

she cried crossly. 'It's much too good for them.' You may believe this threadbare story no more than I do, but nothing could illustrate more neatly the lack of communication between the classes, and its part in the development of censorship.

'Here,' wrote Rose Macaulay in her essay on Reading[1], 'is one of the oddest of the odd conventions which man has sought out, this conveying to one another by marks scratched on paper thoughts privately conceived in the mind. It shows, as all the arts show, the infinite publicism of humankind, the sociability, the interdependence which cannot endure to have a thought, to conceive a tale, a tune, a picture, an arrangement of words, or anything else, but all must forthwith be informed of it.' Printing and reading had long combined as a constant menace to privacy, a compulsive sharing of the facts of life.

On the 13th June, 1643, Cromwell and the Long Parliament reintroduced the licensing system. The following year there appeared the manifesto that will batter its triumphant way into any book about Censorship that expects to be taken seriously:

Areopagitica: a Speech of Mr. John Milton for the Liberty of Unlicensed Printing to the Parliament of England.

Milton was addressing 'the Lords and Commons of England'. It is worth reminding oneself that he was writing 324 years ago. He attacked a new Parliamentary order that 'no book ... shall be henceforth printed unless the same be first approved and licensed by such as shall be thereto appointed'. He reminded his audience that the licensing system was originally introduced by those whom the Puritans most detested – the Papacy and the Inquisition. Freedom in the pursuit of learning, he recalled, had been enjoined by Moses, Daniel, St. Paul and the Fathers, both by precept and by example. 'Promiscuous reading,' he said, 'is necessary to the constituting of human virtue. The attempt to keep out evil doctrine by licensing is like the exploit of that gallant man who thought to keep out the crows by shutting his park gate.' Not only would licensing, i.e. censorship, do no good,

---

1. *Personal Pleasures.* Gollancz, London, 1935.

pleaded Milton, it would be a grave discouragement and affront to learning. And he quoted the case of the imprisoned Galileo, whom he had visited; Galileo who had introduced the concept of time, as a dimension, into philosophy – a space-like dimension that could be measured and divided up into equal parts for the one purpose of making motion amenable to mathematical treatment. Galileo had tried to reconcile Biblical text with his new theories of celestial movement; and, true to what Rose Macaulay has called 'the infinite publicism of mankind', he published his views to the world. He was summoned to Rome and obliged by the Inquisition to abjure his heresies, above all that of the daily and yearly motions of the earth and the stability of the sun. He was required to recite the seven Penitential Psalms once a week for three years. He was also sentenced to be imprisoned for the rest of his life, but this (after much grave hesitation) was not ratified by the Pope.

'Lords and Commons of England,' concluded John Milton, 'consider what nation it is whereof ye are: a nation not slow and dull, but of a quick, ingenious and piercing spirit. It must not be shackled or restricted. Give me the liberty to know, to utter, and to argue freely according to conscience, above all liberties.'

Milton was not heeded in his time: we quote him now as we quote the Cassandras of history, that is to say with half a feeling that they were right then but might be wrong today. The Puritans who saw evil in the pleasures of sex were fundamentalists. 'Who told thee that thou wast naked? Hast thou eaten of the tree whereof I commanded thee that thou shouldest not eat?' And the man said: 'The woman whom thou gavest to be with me, she gave me of the tree . . .' And the Lord God said unto the woman 'I will greatly multiply thy sorrow and thy conception: in sorrow shalt thou bring forth children . . .' It could make the blood run cold at moments when it would normally be warming up. So the Puritans were terrified of any overt biology. Wherever it popped up they struck it smartly on the head. Sex was private; utterly and shamefully secret; best avoided where possible; and where that was reprehensibly not possible, permissible only under a mountain of bedclothes and a tacit pretence that nothing of the kind ever really happened, anywhere.

They sowed a fearful crop of crime, guilt, terror, superstition and insanity. It has flourished and twisted and buried itself in the consciousness of society like some monstrous, ineradicable bindweed.

> In our day [wrote Way in *Man's Quest for Significance*,[1]] sex has been transformed from a source of enjoyment into a neurasthenic complaint. Our sexual troubles have become the full-time occupation of an army of analysts, professors and scientific investigators, and a complete literature of books and pamphlets has grown up to advise people how to manage their instincts. Finally, if this were not enough to witness to the disorder into which our sexual life has fallen, we find sex elevated to the status of a sociological theory which sets out to account in exclusively erotic terms for the whole origin, development and present discontent of civilisation.

Overstatement, no doubt. People persist in enjoying at least one of their sources of neurasthenia. But until the nineteen-forties the isolation of it was still a source of troubled introspection, and it is this isolation that the 'pornographer' has always intensified and exploited. If we stopped calling him names, stopped hating him and supporting him at one and the same time, stopped using the criminal law to show others the consequence of 'eating of the tree', the pornographer might gradually go out of business: a possibility I will return to later.

The Seventeenth-Century Pendulum

Even when the twenty years of repression were over and 'permissiveness' (as we call it now) was changing the course of English literature, the Establishment saw to it that the world was made safe for the new and restored forms of happiness. Milton's *Areopagitica* was not forgotten, but neither was it forgiven. After all, he was a Puritan who had supported

1. Allen and Unwin, London, 1949.

the army against the King. His *Defensio* was burned by the public hangman and he was taken prisoner. The Act of Indemnity saved him, but his plea for liberty 'to argue freely according to conscience' was met by the Licensing Act of 1662, which absolutely (and of course unenforceably) forbade all printing without licence. The Magistrates were empowered to authorise the search of premises and the seizure therein of any unlicensed books. The number of printing firms was limited to twenty. And the opening Section of the new Act said this:

> No person shall presume to print any heretical, seditious, schismatical, or offensive books or pamphlets wherein any doctrine of opinion shall be asserted or maintained which is contrary to the Christian faith, or the doctrine and discipline of the Church of England, or which shall or may tend to be to the scandal of religion, or the Church, or the Government or Governors of the Church, State or Commonwealth or of any corporation or particular person or persons whatever.

There's permissiveness for you. You could not write a book which was 'to the scandal of any person whatever', and you were back with Galileo in what you could say about the Christian dogma. The licence itself, when you got it, went a little further than the provision set out above. It certified that your book said nothing that was 'contrary to good life or good manners, except as the nature of the subject shall require'.

The biological, clerical and philosophical professions, wrote Bernard Shaw in his Preface to Professor R. A. Wilson's *The Miraculous Birth of Language*,[1]

> had been compelled on pain of ostracism and financial ruin to work, write and think on the assumption that the apologues in the book of Genesis are statements of scientific fact, and that the universe is the work of a grotesque tribal idol described in the Book of Numbers as God, who resolves to destroy the human race but is placated by a pleasant smell of roast meat brought to its nostrils by

1. Dent, London, 1937.

Noah. Any baptised and confirmed person questioning this assumption could be and still can be indicted for apostasy and sentenced to penalties as severe as those reserved for manslaughter and treason.[1]

But the licensing authorities were more tolerant about obscenities than even the sixteenth-century Star Chamber, and our bawdiest English playwrights had the time of their lives. So far as one can judge, no one seemed any the worse for it.

Back went the pendulum in 1688. William and Mary might have had a sobering effect anyway, but the political settlement that their arrival represented (to say nothing of the final eclipse of James II) enabled the politicians to give some attention to what the common people were doing. They found that a considerable number of them were reading erotic books and going to Restoration plays. The discovery tended to close the ranks among the upper classes, even Jacobites finding an audience when they attacked the state of public morals – and particularly of the theatre. One angry man, the Rev. Jeremy Collier, stands out above other such writers of the time. He was an extreme High Churchman and a Gray's Inn lecturer in Constitutional Law; and after the Revolution of 1688 he had refused to take the oath of allegiance to William and Mary. When two men who had plotted William's murder were hanged at Tyburn, the Rev. Jeremy Collier gave them absolution on the scaffold without troubling them to confess. For this he was outlawed, and remained an outlaw for the rest of his life, but the condition seems to have been a stimulus to polemical writings of many kinds. Among them was a treatise called *A Short View of the Profaneness and Immorality of the English Stage,* 1968; and this called up against him the angry opposition of the theatrical world, led with skilled invective by Congreve and Vanbrugh. Their contributions to English drama were really the kind of thing that Collier was disturbed about, but the solution

1. Parliament took out this particular provision of the law and looked at it as recently as 1967; but they put it back again. All they did with it (by the Criminal Law Act, 1967, Schedule I) was to take the offence away from Quarter Sessions and make High Court Judges try it.

he proposed was not merely to silence them and their imitators; it was the startlingly simple one of abolishing the theatre altogether.

His point of view was taken up with mild enthusiasm by a number of newly-formed societies for the censoring or suppression of this and that, but their main concern was to punish the anti-religious, the exploiters of prostitution and the now-growing number of drunks. Printed 'obscenity' was still hardly worth bothering about because not enough people could read; but the theatre could bring it home to them too vividly, and the notion of doing away with it was attractive. The next Chapter looks briefly at the theatre's long love-hate relationship with the Lord Chamberlain; and here, by way of preparation for it, is a glimpse of what the Theatres Act of 1968 has done to compensate for his demise. I leave it to theatrical men to guess – at present they can do no more – whether they are going to be better or worse off.

A play is now 'obscene' if, when taken as a whole, 'its effect has a tendency to deprave and corrupt persons who are likely, having regard to all the relevant circumstances, to attend it'. And anyone who puts it on, *whether in public or in private* (except at a rehearsal, at a filming, or 'on a domestic occasion in a private dwelling house' – which won't help the theatre clubs), and *whether for gain or not*, can be prosecuted by the Attorney-General. The defendant can call witnesses to say that the performance was 'justified as being for the public good on the grounds that it was in the interests of drama, opera, ballet or any other art, or of literature or learning'. And the Attorney-General can call witnesses to say it wasn't.

A play given *in public*, whether for gain or not, must not use 'threatening, abusive, or insulting words . . . with intent to stir up hatred against any section of the public distinguished by colour, race or ethnic or national origins'. Theatres will now have to be licensed, in London by the Greater London Council and elsewhere by the local authority. The theatre has, in fact, acquired a host of new censors. A squeamish police superintendent can make a written order *requiring* the management to hand over the script of a play or allow a copy of it to be taken; and any constable, armed with such an order, can make the demand. Whether he has such an order or not he can 'at all reasonable times' go into a licensed theatre to see that the terms of the licence are being complied with.

This has been hailed as 'the end of theatre censorship'.

III

THE DISCOVERY OF
'OBSCENITY'

Eighteenth-century Anxieties about the Stage and the Novel

The police and the Lord Chamberlain have never done very
well in any attempts to enforce obscenity laws against the
theatre, and no doubt this is why they haven't tried very
hard. The Lord Chamberlain's control, which began in
1737 (like that of his predecessor, the Master of the King's
Revels), was the more effective, for it exercised a 'pre-
publication censorship' even more rigorous than the licensing
system for books and newspapers, whereas the police have
always seemed more out of place in the most ribald of theatres
than they do even in a bookshop. In the opening years of the
eighteenth century the effect of Jeremy Collier's denuncia-
tions was still being widely felt, and there were prosecutions
of stage companies for putting on John Crowne's ineffably
boring satirical comedy *Sir Courtly Nice, or It Cannot Be*, Ben
Jonson's *Volpone* (perhaps because Corvino prostitutes his
wife in pursuit of the inheritance – it's hard to find another
reason), Congreve's *Love for Love*, and Vanbrugh's *The
Provoked Wife*. All these prosecutions failed, as they assuredly
would today, when the plays involved are widely considered
narcotic rather than aphrodisiac or debasing.

But the object of the Act of 1737 was mainly political – its
preamble said it was to restrain 'the political and personal
satire' then prevalent on the stage. It set up the Office of
Examiner of Plays, whose last holder has only just relin-
quished powers of censorship and, only too willingly, goes
out with the Theatres Act of 1968. The 1737 Act gave the
Lord Chamberlain total freedom of action – he banned what

he liked or perhaps, since his word was absolute, what he didn't like. (It was not until the Theatres Act of 1843 that his duties were particularised and his decisions thus made susceptible to challenge.) There was even more freedom for the creative writer in plays written merely to be privately and indeed secretly read; and it was not long, accordingly, before their form gave place to that of the novel.

Richardson's *Clarissa Harlowe* was a seven-volume warning about 'the distress that may attend misconduct both of parents and children in relation to marriage', and was a kind of moral sequel to *Pamela*, the first English 'novel of character' (it came out in 1747 and 1748). Mr. Walter Allen, the distinguished literary critic who helped the Society of Authors' Committee in its campaign against the obscenity laws in 1954–59, is in no two minds about *Clarissa Harlowe*, though he is utterly opposed to censorship in all its forms. In his book *The English Novel*[1] he says that Robert Lovelace's erotic treatment of Clarissa is pornography. Compared with it, he thinks, 'the obscenity of Smollett and the indecency of Sterne, so often rebuked by the righteous, appear innocent.' I recall this because of its interesting implication that, in Mr. Allen's view, pornography is rather worse than obscenity or indecency, which can appear innocent by comparison with it. Mr. Geoffrey Gorer, it will be seen from page 43, thinks it is rather better.

Less innocent perhaps but certainly better known are the amorous adventures of *Tom Jones, A Foundling*, which appeared over the name of Henry Fielding in the following year, 1749. Many a modern author whose novel has got him into Court at Bow Street has savoured the irony in the fact that Fielding was appointed Magistrate there in the year before *Tom Jones* was published. Fielding was an old Etonian lawyer-playwright-pamphleteer, and it was he and Richardson who established the form of the English novel. Tom's romping career was much criticised at the time, the affair that gave the most offence being his conquest of Lady Bellaston, to whom he becomes a kind of short-term gigolo. But there was little squeamishness about, and Tobias Smollett and Lawrence Sterne, no less than Richardson and

1. Phoenix House, London, 1954.

Fielding, can be readily acquitted of any charge that their stories were but a primitive framework for a saga of seduction and copulation (which is what the prosecution said *Lady Chatterley's Lover* was). Such an accusation might more truly be levelled at John Cleland's *Fanny Hill, or the Memoirs of a Woman of Pleasure*, which also appeared in 1748; and it is doubtful that he would have attempted to repudiate it. He might well have been surprised if he could have lived to read the publisher's assurance in an edition daringly – and disastrously – published in London in 1963 that 'many eminent' (though anonymous) 'men of letters consider that, in its own right, it is a magnificent work of literature'. This recommendation goes on to say that 'no true picture of the literature of the eighteenth century would be complete without a study of this book'. In 1963 many studies of eighteenth-century English literature began and ended with it. 'A skilful piece of craftsmanship, superior in style and elegance to most of the erotic publications of our own day,' wrote Mr. Louis Untermeyer, the American author and critic; and, when you come to think of the erotic publications, he could have said at least that again.

The other best-known blue book of the eighteenth century was *The List of Covent Garden Ladies*, compiled and published by a Mr. Harris in 1780 in order to supply a channel of advertising for London prostitutes. The fact that he was not prosecuted and that his ladies' directory remained widely accessible may have raised false hopes in the heart of Mr. Frederick Charles Shaw, a publisher of Greek Street, Soho, when he decided to publish his famous *Ladies' Directory* in 1959 – and became one of the first to test the new Obscene Publications Act. To that story we will return, pausing here only to note that the more the erotic appetite changes, the more it remains the same.

Pornography is not Obscenity?

Here a fresh attempt must be made to define pornography. The Act of 1959 actually uses the word in its 'long title', but the long title to a statute is not (yet) any part of the law and its words do not call for definition:

An act to amend the law relating to the publication of obscene matter; to provide for the protection of literature; and to strengthen the law concerning pornography.

But the word does not appear in the text of the Act. 'Obscene' does, and 'literature'; and Sir Alan Herbert wanted it called the Protection of Literature Act – he drafted a Bill of his own to show what he meant, and I hope his biographer is preserving it among the more delightful of the APH memorabilia. The late Lord Birkett, Q.C., offered a definition in an essay written in 1961[1]:

The essence of pornography I take to be the deliberate excitation of sexual feelings; but a book can be obscene, it is said, without any such deliberate purpose.

Yet the deliberate excitation of sexual feelings is the purpose of most fashion design, at least for women; of much of the world's greatest art; of the cosmetics industry; and, it appears, of the pictorial advertising for most commodities and services from toothpaste to North Sea gas.

'Pornography', said the late Sir Herbert Read, 'is a social problem. It is a commodity brought into existence by certain characteristics of a highly developed civilisation. . . . But a *graphic* activity is involved. Whether in literature or in the plastic arts the desired effect is gained by the use of *images*.'[2]

Mr. Geoffrey Gorer says that since pornography is an aspect of literacy, it is confined to the higher civilisations:

It is not a human universal, found in societies of every stage of development as is obscenity. . . . Despite the title of the Obscene Publications Bill, the connections between obscenity and pornography are both tenuous and intermittent. In Latin literature such writers as Juvenal and Martial used the complete obscene vocabulary without, apparently, being considered pornographic. . . . Conversely, to the best of my recollection *Fanny Hill* (one of the few masterpieces of English pornography) does not use a single obscene term.

Mr. Gorer's definition of pornography is of a clarity that I do not remember to have seen equalled. He ends by saying

1. & 2. *Does Pornography Matter?* Routledge, London, 1961.

that 'in its most usual form it is a fiction, in prose or verse, narrative or dialogue, mainly or entirely concerned with the sexual activities of the imagined characters.' Dr. Robert Gosling sees it as

> erotic material whether visual or verbal that is believed to have a corrupting influence, rightly or wrongly in the event. . . . Alternatively, one might define it as all the visual material that at the present time and in a particular society is judged by the authorities as impermissibly erotic.[1]

The word itself, wrote Dom Denys Rutledge, is to most people unpleasing and evil-sounding, 'so that they hesitate to use it in public or say it only in a whisper, or look round first to see if children are present'.

> In the mind of the scholar responsible for the word in the big *Oxford Dictionary* (adds Father Rutledge) there seems to have been present a suspicion that it carried the idea of *inciting* to unchaste and lewd behaviour, for he quotes *Webster* as offering the murals at Pompeii, in rooms designed for the Bacchanalian orgies, as examples of pornography.[2]

So it is the presentation, he concludes, through words or the visual arts, of the unchaste. And he makes the profound observation that the portrayal of what is good and beautiful in sex may 'corrupt' as easily as the portrayal of the un- chaste – 'perhaps more easily since it is always the positive good in an act which through external circumstances is evil that attracts. Man can never be attracted by evil as such.'

All of which is important in considering the development of printed and pictorial pornography as an industry. I propose to accept the separation of pornography from obscenity, practically as well as etymologically (which now hardly matters at all). In Europe and America some aspects of sexuality can be obscene though among tribes with fertility cults they may be sacred. There are private acts and functions with no sexual content that would be publicly obscene, though they could never entice, or incite, or tempt anyone into doing anything he should not do and might even make him sick.

1 and 2. *Does Pornography Matter?* Routledge, London, 1961.

So it was pornography rather than obscenity that took an immense modern impetus from the secondary education that was made statutorily compulsory in England in 1902. Since 1896 Northcliffe's *Daily Mail* had been building up a habitual mass readership (as well as his weekly journals), upon whom the pornographers gradually moved in. It was very largely adolescent, an audience of schoolboys; and some of them were very probably harmed by it in so far as they were being introduced to the greatest human love sacrament as though it were the bearded lady in a side-show. It is known that the pornographic books and magazines also reach a large number of lonely middle-aged and elderly men, to whom it would seem they can do no conceivable harm and to whom they may possibly afford a solace and relief that is free from harm to others. The trade built up until at the middle of the century a large industry was thriving on it, many of the publications and periodicals being covert subsidiaries of publishing houses that were always ready to disown them. There was money in twentieth-century pornography, but there was risk as well.

By 1956, when the Select Committee on the Obscene Publications Bill was receiving evidence, the Home Office was able to supply the following figures (I have selected those given for the five-year period then concluded):

	1952	1953	1954	1955	1956
Number of 'destruction orders' made	115	154	132	38	38

Number of articles ordered to be destroyed:					
Books and magazines	31,842	44,130	167,293	3,056	2,110
Photographs	8,329	20,141	10,803	7,142	3,019
Postcards	16,029	32,603	16,646	1,214	22,558
Miscellaneous	2,546	1,950	18,609	151	1,745

	1952	1953	1954	1955	1956
Persons found guilty of publishing obscene books	34	49	111	43	42
Total amount of Fines	£906	£2,786	£12,677	£1,830	£1,724
Range of prison sentences	6 to 18 months	3 to 12 months	3 to 18 months	2 weeks to 3 years	2 months to 1 year

The heavy figures for 1954, which was also the year of the 'big five' prosecutions (see page 93), were largely due to the seizure by the police of 108,000 copies of a book ordered by a stipendiary magistrate to be destroyed as obscene.

And in 1963, four years after the Obscene Publications Act came into operation, the Deputy Director of Public Prosecutions, addressing a public meeting on 'Pornography as Big Business'[1], said that the Soho bookshops engaged in this particular trade were then 'taking as much as £100 a day – that is £30,000 a year.' Referring in particular to obscene paper back 'novels' imported from America he said this:

> A few years ago there were practically none. That was because there was until 1961 a prohibition of the importation – except under licence – of American printed matter unless the article was in excess of a fixed value. In 1961 the restrictions on dollar imports were relaxed. Between 1961 and 1963 the Police and Customs between them actually seized 1,863,000 obscene novels. ... Of course, when I say imported I am speaking only of those which were either seized by the Customs on entry or subsequently seized by the police. It is difficult to hazard a guess what the actual figure is, but one would think the police and customs were lucky if, between them, they

1. Reproduced in *Pornography and Public Morals.* Public Morality Council, London, 1963.

managed to seize more than one in every half-dozen
imported into this country.

Which would produce a total of about 12 million obscene
imported novels. The Deputy D.P.P. added that 'pin-up
magazines' were published mainly in the United Kingdom
and that the extent of the trade could be judged from the
fact that on one raid in November 1963, the police seized
over eight tons of them. 'The printers and publishers are
changing every day,' he said, 'and the police find that their
efforts to stem the tide of these magazines are rather like
those of Canute.'

The Wily Business Man

The Obscene Publications Act of 1964 amended the 1959
Act so as to catch the wholesaler, from whom no one other
than the retail dealer, and certainly not a policeman, would
be likely to obtain a book or magazine. It did this by making
it an offence merely to *have* an obscene article for publication
for gain. But the police now complain that it took away with
one hand what it had given them with the other: it provides
that the wholesaler – or anyone else – is not to be convicted

> if he proves that he had not examined the article and had
> no reasonable cause to suspect that it was such that his
> having it could make him liable to be convicted of an
> offence.

This was a present to the pornographer, wholesale or retail.
'The wily business man in the pornographic trade,' said the
Deputy D.P.P. in the speech already quoted (a man in the
wrong kind of business is always wily) 'is well aware of this
defence.'

> He makes full use of it in this way. The American publishers
> send him quantities of books without invoicing them by
> their titles. They are merely ordered in bulk and shipped
> in bulk, and the documents don't show the titles or the
> nature of the books consigned.

It doesn't seem particularly wily, and in fact it was being
done before the special defence was provided by law. But

there is reason to believe that some aspects of the trade are
more prosperous than ever; and it is a trade that derives a
fresh stimulus from every effort to stamp it out by police
action. The comparison with Canute may be a better one
than it had seemed to the Deputy D.P.P. (page 47); for that
wise King was concerned to show his sycophantic courtiers
not that he could control the tides but that they were
invincible and that he had got his feet wet. The police may
be doing much the same thing.

IV

THE NINETEENTH CENTURY
'READERSHIP EXPLOSION'

The Public Libraries and the 'Vice Societies'

The Victorians are too close to us to be written about with the confidence that informs the histories of the Middle Ages. My mother remembered the 1870 Siege of Paris and Forster's Education Act, the publication of *Through the Looking Glass*, Booth founding the Salvation Army in 1878. In 1879, my father was brought home from Zululand as an orphan of nine because his father had died in the massacre of the 10th Regiment of Foot at Isandhlwana. Both parents lived to a great age and remembered Victorian England vividly. It was a different England from the one I now read about, in books written by men half my age. As my parents' ageing memories reached the curious condition in which the events of last week are forgotten and those of 75 years ago become crystal clear, I encouraged them to remember and talk. My picture seems more vivid than the one I get from the social histories.

The Victorians may have done a little less reading than we do but they lived in what they read, identifying themselves with the fictional characters invented in such vast numbers for them. They had little leisure. (My parents seem to have had none.) They got into trouble less, partly because there was less time for mischief, partly because the police seldom seemed to catch anyone but the most ostentatious blackguards and the horizontal (and multitudinous) drunks. The Victorians found time, as men and women have found time since the Creation, for much sexual promiscuity; a dead baby in the street was as common a sight then as an abandoned car is now, and everyone, charitably assuming that it was illegitimate, passed by on the other side. There was much exhortation from pulpits and from leader columns. And there were the Vice Societies.

The most energetic of these was the Society for the Suppression of Vice founded as far back as 1803 as a successor to William Wilberforce's 'Proclamation Society'. The Wilberforce idea had been to revive and implement a Proclamation issued about 30 years earlier by George III, which included a requirement that all good citizens should unite to condemn

> loose and licentious prints, books and publications, dispensing poison to the minds of the young and unwary; and to punish the publishers and the vendors thereof.

Both the Archbishops and all the Bishops supported it. In many ways it resembled today's Social Morality Council (formerly the Public Morality Council), from whose annual reports the following passage might well have been taken – instead it is from the Proclamation Society's report for 1800:

> The publication of obscene books and prints is an offence which attracted the Society's earliest attention, and to which as an object of the first importance it has uniformly continued to direct its regard.

The writers of obscene books had thus taken precedence in the Society's demonology over the opponents of Sunday observance, atheistic propagandists (the Society had many conflicts with the irreverent Richard Carlile, though even he supported its campaign against obscenity), fortune-tellers, brothels, disorderly theatres and music-halls. The Society was supported, at least in its censorship campaign, by Joseph Hume, Francis Place – and Dr. Thomas Bowdler.

Dr. Bowdler, editor of the *Family Shakespeare*, was a scholar of immense industry whose name has become a traditional joke. 'Nothing,' he said in the Preface to his ten-volume Shakespeare, 'is added to the original text, but those words and expressions are omitted which cannot with propriety be read aloud in a family.' Bowdlerising has angered generations of purists, but the Shakespeare texts we had at school owed much to him – without acknowledgment, which would have made them unsaleable among the headmasters and education committees. 'No man ever did better service to Shakespeare,' wrote Swinburne in *Studies in Prose and Poetry*, 1894, 'than the man who made it possible to put him into the hands of intelligent and imaginative children.' And Swinburne knew what expurgation could do to a man's work.

In spite of it all, or perhaps because of it, pornography poured from the printing presses – long erotic novels of absolutely no survival value, whose heroes staggered from one bed to another; weekly and monthly magazines which pandered to all those appetites that the 'Vice Societies' were working vainly to eliminate. There was a huge flagellation literature (to which Swinburne enthusiastically contributed), and it appeared in many guises and at every kind of cost. The 'readership explosion' had taken the class out of pornography and merely rearranged its prices to suit all purses.

A small proportion of all these publications was being imported from France. Its significance was exaggerated because the arbitrary powers of the Customs authorities made it a little easier to control than the indigenous product; and by making a fuss of it the law could seem to be doing rather better than it really was. By 1853 a Customs Consolidation Act had been passed to deal more effectively – by seizing them at the ports – with 'indecent or obscene prints, paintings, books, cards, lithographic or other engravings or any other indecent or obscene articles'. Twenty-three years later a further 'Consolidation Act' repeated this list of undesirables and merely added photographs – by that time the 'Paris photograph' had already become famous. By this Act of 1876 (as now re-enacted in 1952) the Customs Officers can seize 'obscenities' they find being imported and give notice to the bearer or to the consignee that this has been done. (They do it orally if he is there at the time.) He is allowed one month to contest the seizure if he wants to. Usually he doesn't, but contrary to what seems to be the general belief it is for the Customs authorities, if he does contest it in writing, to take the matter to Court. They

call it 'taking condemnation proceedings'. The proceedings
are civil, not criminal, and the burden of proof (which is
rather less heavy than if they *were* criminal) rests on the
Customs men. *But* they can prosecute criminally if they think
the case is a bad one, and the maximum penalties would then
be £100 or three times the value of the seized book or books,
plus two years' imprisonment – the longest prison sentence
that Magistrates are authorised to impose. The Solicitor to
the Commissioners of Customs and Excise, Mr. M. G.
Whittome, told the Select Committee of 1956 that 'in
practice, individuals importing obscene matter in single
copies for personal use would *not* be prosecuted although the
matter would be seized'.[1] If the seizure is not contested, or it
is contested unsuccessfully, the 'obscene matter' is destroyed.
(But specimen and marked copies are kept: the Customs
Officers don't want to read all the way through again, when
another copy turns up in someone's luggage.)

The Obscene Publications Act 1857

Then in 1857 Lord Campbell produced his famous Bill
empowering the Magistrates to order the destruction of books
and prints (found in this country, not imported ones) if
they believed that publication of them would amount to 'a
misdemeanour proper to be prosecuted'. A magistrate
could issue a search warrant on being shown a copy of the
offending book or article; and usually the police would then
expect to come back to him with a lot more. Some mixed
bags have been placed before magistrates after searches of
this kind. Among hundreds, or perhaps, thousands of 'girlie'
magazines and non-seaside postcards there may be one or
two good novels containing words that have shocked the
police, accustomed as the police are to seeing them only on
walls or hearing them in mess-room adjudications on rival
footballers; and until *Lady Chatterley's Lover* was vindicated in
1960, the appearance of that book among seized magazines
had been enough to get a number of small booksellers into
prison. Introducing his Bill in the House of Lords in 1857,
Lord Campbell said it was

1. Minutes of Evidence, *House of Commons Paper* No. 122 of 1956, p. 48.

intended to apply exclusively to works *written for the single purpose of corrupting the morals of youth*, and of a nature calculated to shock the common feelings of decency in a well regulated mind. . . . When there are people who designedly and industriously manufacture books and prints *with the intention of corrupting morals, and when they succeed in their infamous purpose*, I think it is necessary for the legislature to interpose.

I have italicised the phrases that show how far this Act was from reality, and yet how little its Parliamentary purpose has been studied in the course of its enforcement. Purpose, and intention, and success in sowing corruption, have played next to no part in the many trials to which the Act has given rise. Myriads of books have been burned because magistrates have felt their own well-regulated minds to be shocked. Yet Lord Campbell was no kill-joy, at least in relation to the youthful pleasures of the well-to-do. He thought you could have well-regulated fun – fun so long as you kept it within bounds. According to Hardcastle's biography of him he once said this in extenuation of the roisterer:

I cannot help thinking that an occasional booze has a favourable tendency to excite the faculties (I wonder what faculties his Lordship had in mind?), to warm the affections, to improve the manners, and to form the character of youth. Of course it is to be understood that excess is to be avoided, which is not only contrary to morality but inconsistent with true enjoyment.

Only ten years went by before this Act was called into use in a story that put *Hicklin's* Case into the law books of the entire English-speaking world. The Wolverhampton Magistrates had made an order for the destruction of 252 copies of an anti-papist pamphlet on the ground that it was obscene. The owner of the pamphlets, Mr Henry Scott, who had bought them to distribute as a good Anglican, was therefore the 'publisher'. He appealed to Wolverhampton Quarter Sessions, where the Recorder allowed his appeal on the ground that the pamphlet was concerned only to 'expose' the Church of Rome and not to harm anyone's morals. The learned Recorder's name was Hicklin; and when the prosecution, having decided to appeal further to the High

Court, asked Mr Hicklin to 'state a case for the consideration of a Queen's Bench Divisional Court', they launched it into legal history as *Hicklin's* Case. The Judges of the Queen's Bench Divisional Court, led by Chief Justice Cockburn, reversed Mr. Hicklin's decision in a judgment that sent the words 'tendency to deprave and corrupt' on their 100-years' odyssey through the criminal courts.

The Common Law – Revival or Innovation?

But merely destroying books and pamphlets was thought not to satisfy the public feeling, or at least the judicial feeling, that someone must also be seen to be punished. There had to be some prosecutions, fines and imprisonments. On what authority? Parliament in 1857 had said nothing about punishing anyone, apart from burning his books, which seldom ruined him.

So the Common Law was invoked, 'the law of the land from time immemorial', from before the birth of Parliament; some of which is supposed to reside 'in the bosoms of the Judges' (*in gremio judicum*). Not that the law of libel came down from time immemorial. Its attempted application to obscenity had failed 150 years earlier in the case of *R. v. Read* (1708). Read had published a book called *The Fifteen Plagues of a Maidenhead*, and although the Judge said it was 'stuff not fit to be mentioned publicly', he added that 'if there is no remedy in the Spiritual Court, it does not follow that there must be a remedy here. There is no law to punish it – I wish there were, but we cannot make law.'

But they took only 20 years to get over this shyness about 'making law'. This time the offender was Edward Curll, bookseller, pamphleteer – and pornographer. Pope had a dig at him in Book 1 of *The Dunciad*:

> Hence bards, like Proteus long in vain tied down,
> Escape in monsters and amaze the town.
> Hence Miscellanies spring, the weekly boast
> Of Curll's chaste press and Lintot's rubric post.[1]

1. Lintot was another bookseller and publisher. His name on his bookshop was in vivid red lettering.

And in 1727 Edward Curll had published the book that the law seemed to have been waiting for. It was called *Venus in the Cloister, or the Nun in Her Smock*. It was a bit too much. This kind of thing *must* be wrong and, if the law didn't say so, it had better start saying so now. What we now call 'the public good' was then known as 'the King's Peace', a concept as old as Saxon law. It wasn't always in operation throughout the country or all the time – it had once been confined to regally favoured areas and to holy seasons. And it used to die with the King. Thus when Henry I died 'there was seen tribulation in the land, for every man that could forthwith robbed another' (according to a chronicler quoted in *Kenny's Outlines of Criminal Law*). When Edward I was away at the Crusades and his father died, the nobles at home took it upon themselves to proclaim 'the King's Peace' by way of preserving order. Any criminal offence whatsoever (according to recent editions of *Kenny*) can be a 'breach of the Queen's peace'; and for centuries the Judges could decide what was such a breach and what wasn't.

In Edward Curll's case they decided that the publication of *Venus in the Cloister* was a breach of George II's peace. They fined Curll and made him stand in the pillory. Only one of the Judges seemed to think (as more of us would think today) that a 'breach of the peace' ought to be something in the nature of a public uproar, with police helmets flying and innocent bystanders being 'flung into police vans'. The rest of the King's Bench took the view put to them by the Attorney-General:

This is an obscene libel, and an offence at Common Law. It tends to corrupt the morals of the King's subjects. Peace includes good order and government, and it may be broken in many instances without any actual force – first, if it be an act against the constitution of civil government; secondly, if it be against religion; thirdly, if against morality. I do not insist that every immoral act is indictable, such as telling a lie or the like; but if it is destructive of morality in general, if it does or may affect all the King's subjects, then it is an offence of a public nature. Upon this distinction it is that particular acts of fornication are not punishable in the temporal courts, and bawdy houses are.

Thus the idea of 'obscene libel' had arrived. Not in the sense of private libel, which is always defamatory and is of two kinds, civil and criminal – depending on the remedy sought by the victim, i.e., whether damages for himself or punishment for his traducer. Obscene libel was one of the 'public libels', the others (both now obsolescent) being blasphemous and seditious. The idea that a libel could be 'for the public good' was recognised by Parliament a century later, when the Libel Act of 1843 said that anyone *prosecuted for defamatory libel* who wanted to run the defence that what he had written was true (the 'plea of justification') would have to prove also that its publication was 'for the public good'.

The Growing Love of Reading

Curll's case had led to no witch-hunt, encouraged no spate of prosecutions. Even Wilkes's *Essay on Woman*, surely an obscene publication by the standard adopted in Curll's case, was prosecuted for political reasons only (1763). But although in this perennial publisher-v.-censor game it is always easy to confuse cause and effect, there did ensue throughout the nineteenth century a torrent of mainly decorous literature – from Dickens, Lytton, Dumas, Disraeli, Lear, the Brontës, Thackeray, Mrs. Gaskell, Kingsley, Hawthorne, Borrow, Trollope, Charles Reade, Meredith, Wilkie Collins, Mrs. Henry Wood, Lewis Carroll, Ouida, Alcott, Henry James, Stevenson.

It was the great age of readers, the greatest of all for writers. Virginia Woolf, in our time, could speak of a Victorian childhood. 'I have sometimes dreamt', she wrote,

> that when the Day of Judgement dawns and the great conquerors and lawyers and statesmen come to receive their reward – their crowns, their laurels, their names carved indelibly upon imperishable marble – the Almighty will turn to Peter and will say, not without a certain envy, when He sees *us* coming with our books under our arms, 'Look, these need no reward. We have nothing to give them here. They have loved reading.'

The love of reading was almost universal. Did the Judges' discovery of 'obscene libel' proceed from a public longing for

books of the 'family reading' kind, or was that longing a
timid and obedient outcome of the Judges' discovery? It is
possible at least to maintain that Victorian authors and
publishers, overshadowed by a large warning notice that
they had better find other appetites and adventures to depict
than the sexuality of man, tried harder to find them than
publishers have tried at any other period in our literary
history. They found them too. Though the sexuality was
going on in no small way all the time, most of the authors
I have just named wrote as though sexuality was something
to be no more than hinted at; and the consequent stimulus
to their non-erotic inventiveness coincided with the great age
of the English novel. I draw no inferences.

The French Invasion

But just occasionally a publisher rebelled, keeping the law
from falling fast asleep. The works of Balzac, Zola, Baroche,
Sainte-Beuve and other Frenchmen who had never heard of
'The Queen's Peace', the Common Law, or obscene libel,
were imported in considerable quantities. From about 1870
onwards there was a mounting campaign in the press, not
only in the numerous religious papers but in the sober literary
reviews, against these polluters of the stream of English
literature of the time. Henry Vizetelli, a London bookseller
and publisher of Italian extraction, had published Edgar
Allan Poe's *Tales of Mystery and Imagination* and works as
morally unassailable as *Uncle Tom's Cabin*. He began to
publish translations of Sand, Daudet, Prosper Merimée,
Maupassant, Gautier, Balzac, Flaubert, and finally Zola.
Zola proved to be too much, especially *La Terre* (even though
Vizetelli had 'Bowdlerised' it for delicate English readers).
Too much, that is to say, for the National Vigilance Association, not for the police or the Home Office. The Association
took out a summons against Henry Vizetelli for 'uttering
and publishing certain obscene libels, to wit, certain books
entitled *La Terre* by Emile Zola, *Madame Bovery* by Gustave
Flaubert, *Sappho* by Alphonse Daudet, *Bel Ami* by Guy de
Maupassant, and *Madame de Maupin* by Theophile Gautier,

against the Peace of Our Sovereign Lady The Queen, her Crown and Dignity.' The trial came on at the Old Bailey on the 31st October, 1888, and began with a furious row about the language of the prosecution (now rather reluctantly taken over by the Crown) in diminishing the status of Emile Zola as a writer. When prosecuting Counsel was reading aloud the passages that the jury were expected to find obscene, a member of the jury objected to having to listen to them.

Well, what would *you* do in Vizetelli's place? You start with a jury that can't even bear to hear the words you've offered? The words of a man who, two weeks earlier, had been appointed to the French Legion of Honour for his services to literature and freedom. He gave up the case. He changed his plea to Guilty and the trial was over before it had really begun. The Court felt more merciful than it does when a publisher or bookseller insists that his book is *not* obscene and fights the case to the end. Would Mr. Vizetelli promise to withdraw all his Zola books from circulation? So far as he could, Yes. So he was discharged. The very next year he was in the dock again over some more of his French novels, and this time the Judge gave him three months' imprisonment.

Havelock Ellis

Ten years later (1898) there appeared the first volume in Dr Havelock Ellis's *Studies in the Psychology of Sex*. It was called *Sexual Inversion* and it dealt, clinically and dispassionately, with homosexuality. It may have been a little unfortunate that the timidity of English publishers had obliged Havelock Ellis to resort to a crook pornographic publisher called Villiers (he had a dozen aliases and his real name is now in doubt); but it was a major misfortune for Ellis that only three years earlier (1895) the sensational trials of Oscar Wilde had convinced the British public that Justinian was right – homosexuality was so evil that it was the cause of earthquakes.

Havelock Ellis was a writer of grace and distinction – he was said to have 'the patience of a Darwin, the brilliance of a Huxley, the style of a Macaulay.' He was revered in medical circles long after the advent of Freud, whose theories soon became the more generally popular for their liberating effect on the conscience. The prosecution could have been the occasion of a major change in the law which, as it turned out, was to be delayed another 60 years, namely the decision that expert evidence should be admissible to prove a book's scientific merits. The defence assembled a team of experts, precisely as in the *Chatterley* case in 1960. The Judge (the Recorder at the Old Bailey) *might* have refused to hear them, as the Bow Street Magistrate was to refuse 30 years later in the case against Radclyffe Hall's *Well of Loneliness* (see p. 79). No doubt there was present to all the engaged legal minds the opinion of that great nineteenth-century lawyer Sir James FitzJames Stephen, that the publication of an 'obscene libel' could be 'for the public good' (see p. 27), an idea taken over from the established defence of 'justification' in a prosecution for defamatory libel. But the problem, alas, did not arise. The defendant in this case was not Dr. Havelock Ellis but the bookseller who had been selling *Sexual Inversion* – Thomas Bedborough. To the dismay of everyone else the bookseller at the last minute – as has happened in so many cases since – pleaded Guilty; and the case was over without a word of evidence.

> 'I am willing to believe', the Recorder told Bedborough magnanimously, binding him over not to do it again, 'that in acting as you did you might at the first outset perhaps have been gulled into the belief that somebody might say this was a scientific work. But it is impossible for anybody with a head on his shoulders to open the book without seeing that it is a pretence and a sham, and that it is merely entered into for the purpose of selling this obscene publication.'

The assembled medical witnesses, all of whom had heads on their shoulders, went disconsolately away, their evidence unheard. Unheard also, Havelock Ellis was condemned in the public mind as what he bitterly called 'a purveyor of literary garbage'. He had no right to speak, he could not be heard because he was not a defendant; and if a thousand booksellers took the same course and branded his book a thousand times, his position would always be the same.

So it would today. The law officers of the Crown and the Home Office legal advisers steadfastly resisted all attempts, during the debates on the 1959 Bill, to give the author, publisher and printer the right to be joined as a defendant when a bookseller is *prosecuted* (as distinct from having his books destroyed). The Select Committee thought this right *should* be accorded:

> The Society of Authors pressed strongly for a provision giving a right to the author to be heard in any proceedings where he was *not* himself a party, although they admitted that his status would constitute a novelty in legal procedure. . . . We appreciate the force of the arguments put forward. Two fundamental liberties are involved. The first is freedom of expression: a reputable author will wish both to stand by what he has written and to defend his writing against attack in any form, but he may be denied the opportunity to do so under the present law. Secondly, the writer of a book has a form of property in the continued circulation of his work, but he may find that he is unable to intervene in a trial where both his royalties and his reputation may be adversely affected. Similar considerations apply in the case of the publisher and printer.

So they recommended that in 'destruction order proceedings', the author, publisher and printer should be given a right to be heard 'unless the person summoned objects'. In the event the 1959 Act gave them the right whether the person summoned objected or not. (The only reason why the person summoned might object is that he wants to get it all over quickly and cheaply: but the co-defendants could be made to pay their share of the cost – or even more. Anyway, Parliament swept the objection aside.) But the Select Committee also recommended that the same right should accrue in the case of a *prosecution* – e.g., as in the Havelock Ellis case:

> In the case of a criminal prosecution . . . the author, publisher, printer and bookseller may well be accused jointly, but this will not necessarily be so.[1] We consider that if he is not already charged the author should be given a right to be heard provided that the defence has no objection.

1. In practice they never are.

Parliament would have none of it. They could not see what *locus standi* would be enjoyed by people who volunteered to appear, and they would not 'tie the hands of the prosecuting authorities' as to whom they should bring compulsorily to Court as defendants. So the Havelock Ellis situation could – though it will probably not – happen all over again. His book, however, has since been translated into dozens of languages – 'to reach people', he wrote in later years, 'who could not say what a Recorder is. . . . Unto this day it continues to bring me from many lands the reverent and grateful words of strangers, whose praise keeps me humble in the face of the supreme mystery of life.'

On which note the story of the literary censorship in Britain may perhaps be ushered hopefully into the twentieth century.

V

EVENTS OF THE
TWENTIETH CENTURY

The New Non-System

You might have thought that the discovery, or re-discovery, of the Common Law offence of obscene libel would have settled the pattern of Crown policy at long last, in relation to 'obscenity' and the printed word. When the police now seized a quantity of obscene or pornographic 'rubbish', being authorised to do so by a magistrate who had seen a sample of it, they would merely ask him for a destruction order. No one would be accused of anything; there would be no 'prosecution', but the books would be got out of the way with a minimum of trouble. When the police came across a book which, though it seemed to them obscene or pornographic, contained long words, Latin phrases or footnotes about *The Golden Bough* or *The Anatomy of Melancholy*, that would be a matter for a jury and so there would be a prosecution against the publisher and sometimes the author.

But in fact no such pattern emerged. Not all the pin-up merchants (who today are almost immune but who were then considered quintessentially evil) were disposed of by magistrates' orders. Some of them were committed for trial by juries. As recently as the nineteen-fifties they were being sent to prison. If you go round some of the prisons today you will see the walls of cells and workshops decorated with the very pin-ups they went to prison for publishing.

In 1961, at Surrey Quarter Sessions, a commercial magazine publisher was sent to prison for 9 months for publishing an illustrated booklet called 'Scanties', though it could not have conceivably 'corrupted' anyone. He appealed to the Court of Criminal Appeal on the ground that the Judge who had tried him had not told the jury they should be satisfied the article was 'something more than shocking and vulgar'. The Lord Chief Justice said, in effect, that it didn't matter what the Judge had or had not told his jury; you only had to pick the thing up to feel 'quite certain that no jury could conceivably have failed to convict'.[1] Today, only seven years later, no such prosecution would be brought, or even imagined, no jury would convict if it were, and no Court of Appeal Bench would be happy to let the conviction stand if they did. It is fair to say that even then the Judges reduced the penalty from 9 months' imprisonment to a fine of £500.[2] But why wasn't the case brought, if it had to be brought at all, by way of an application for a magistrate's destruction order? No evidence of system here.

There *had* been attempts at uniformity of procedure. A Joint Select Committee of both Lords and Commons in 1908 had urged that all the Acts of Parliament dealing with pornography should be repealed and that one consolidating Statute should make all the relevant offences 'summary', i.e., disposable by magistrates. This would have got rid of jury trial in obscenity 'first offences'. It proposed that magistrates could levy fines up to £30 (or a month's imprisonment) for a first offence, and £100 or six months if it was a second offence or involved a person under 16; and the six months' liability would have conferred a right to jury trial *if wanted*. This was a formula that had been found successful in the case of the Street Betting Act of 1906. The anxiety at that time seemed to be to keep these cases away from juries, and magistrates were to be specifically entrusted with the decision whether the book was redeemed as 'a book of literary merit or a genuine work of art'. A magistrate was *not* to listen to expert evidence, about the literary or artistic merits any more than about the obscenity. It is worth recalling that 1908 was a 'Liberal' year (Lloyd George took over in April from Campbell-Bannerman), as well as a vintage literary year, among the books published in the course of it

1. Compare this with what the Court of Appeal said about 'instructing juries' in the *Last Exit to Brooklyn* case (p. 114).

2. *R.* v. *Clifford, The Times*, 18th April, 1961.

being Bennett's *Old Wives' Tale*, Chesterton's *The Man who was Thursday*, W. H. Davies' *Autobiography of a Super Tramp*, E. M. Forster's *A Room with a View*, Anatole France's *Penguin Island*, and Kenneth Grahame's *The Wind in the Willows*.

The Select Committee's recommendations produced only one result, but it was rather important: they wanted an international convention among as many nations as possible – there was not yet any League of Nations – to exchange information about and assist in the suppression of obscene literature; and such a convention, signed in 1910, became the basis for the U.N. Convention Relating to the Suppression of the Circulation of and Trade in Obscene Publications; this was concluded at Geneva on 12th September 1923, and ratified by Great Britain on 11th December 1925.[1] Significantly, each country reserved the right to define 'obscenity' in its own way; and even so Denmark, renouncing the Convention in 1967, drastically amended its own obscenity laws so that now, for the modern Dane, *almost* anything goes. (And, incidentally, after an initial boom in pornography the Danish branch of the business is said to be in despondent decline.)

Meanwhile the policy of the British police, the Director of Public Prosecutions and the Judges, vacillating between the book-burning and the imprisoning (or fining), went on exhibiting no kind of pattern. In 1915 D. H. Lawrence's *The Rainbow* was burned (to the tune of 1,000 copies) without any prosecution – or, therefore, any chance of its adequate defence[2]; and in the same year there were jury trials involving totally unmemorable 'novels' and magazines, which were defended vigorously and in some cases successfully. Joyce's *Ulysses* was left alone, though its importation in single copies from France (where it was published in 1922) was being achieved through many stratagems, including that of binding it up in the covers of a *cordon bleu* cookery book. Radclyffe Hall's *The Well of Loneliness*, which almost any jury must surely have acquitted, was disposed of in 1928 by getting a destruction order from the Bow Street magistrate – who refused to hear any 'expert' evidence (see p. 79).

1. Treaty Series No. 1, 1926: Cmd. 2575.
2. *The Rainbow* case is further discussed on p. 70.

The Police 'Disclaimer' Form

What did evolve from all this during the 1940s was the 'disclaimer' system invented by the Metropolitan Police, enabling them to destroy books that no one would bother to defend in Court. It was fifteen years before this came officially to light (during the enquiries of the Select Committee on the 1959 Bill); and it is important enough to merit a digression here. Ten years ago there was a disposition to regard it as something rather sinister, arbitrary and anti-democratic. It was, however, little more sinister than the ten shilling fine on a parking ticket. The Metropolitan Police told the Select Committee[1] that in 1956 they executed 34 search warrants, applied for only two destruction orders, and 'acted upon' 77 'disclaimers'. The form of disclaimer said: 'I . . . do hereby disclaim ownership to the above . . . items shown in a list of property seized by police from my bookshop at . . . on . . . 19 . . .'

> This practice (said the police in their evidence to the Committee) has been in use for many years. It has the advantage of saving time – i.e., no summons is issued or served, and there is no hearing before a magistrate and no examination of documents by a magistrate. Naturally, if a person wants to dispute the matter, he does not sign a disclaimer, and a 'summons to show cause' is issued. As to the attitude of the Courts, there were two cases in 1952 when a 'summons to show cause' had been issued, and at the hearing of each case it was announced by the Magistrate that the defendants had written to the Court stating that they did not object to the destruction of the material; and, in view of that, he did not propose to examine it. The summons was adjourned *sine die*. The police obtained a disclaimer; and then they destroyed all the articles.

Not that the idea was new, the Committee were told by one of the police witnesses, or that it was even confined to obscene or indecent articles. 'It often happens that we find indecent material on persons who are interviewed in the course of routine enquiries: they voluntarily (*sic*) surrender that stuff to the particular police officer, and in those instances there

1. *Minutes of Evidence Taken Before the Select Committee on the Obscene Publications Bill*, 1958, No. 122, p. 74.

is no legal power to seize it from them, and there is no other
way of dealing with it, except by getting the person concerned to sign a disclaimer that he no longer wants it and
that the police can destroy it.'[1]

This police witness explained in answer to a barrage of
questions that if the police did take the matter to court, 'very
frequently the owner of the material wrote in at the last
minute and said he didn't want to dispute the proceedings.
That left the magistrate with the stuff there and nobody to
dispute it.' Committee members seemed to think it relatively
unimportant that the magistrate should have undisputed
books or pictures on his hands and not know what to do with
them. If he thought they *ought* to be disputed, that must
mean that he thought them innocuous; so why not order
their return to the owner? If he thought them obscene he
should order their destruction. Mr. Roy Jenkins was one
member who didn't like it much:

> 'In the vast majority of cases it means that the police and
> not the Courts decide what is to be destroyed?'
> 'I don't think so,' replied the Commissioner, Sir John
> Nott-Bower, 'because nobody is under any sort of com-
> pulsion to sign a form like that, nor is he under any sort of
> misapprehension. If anybody doesn't like the idea of
> signing a disclaimer, then of course we can proceed by way
> of summons in the ordinary way.'
> 'But if you had 77 disclaimers in 1956, and only two
> destruction orders, it *was* the police and not the courts who
> decided?'[2]

No, said the Commissioner, it was the owner, and his
agreement was 'entirely voluntary'. The Commissioner
agreed with a reminder from Mr. Roy Jenkins (recalling
earlier police evidence) that 'disclaimers' might be used
when someone was being questioned about an entirely
different crime and was found to be in possession of 'indecent
material'.

> 'Without the use of the disclaimer there would be no legal
> means of getting that material?'
> 'No.'

1. *Ibid.* p. 78. Q. 538.
2. *Ibid.* Q. 547/8.

But why, persisted Mr. Roy Jenkins, did the police *want* to take indecent material from people – material they had no legal right to take? Well, these people usually got it through the post, and the suppliers had large mailing lists, and the man being interviewed might be on such a list and be useful as a witness. 'In addition', said the Commissioner of Police, 'they might have other indecent material, and it is the practice to ask them whether they wish to retain it: and if they say "No", the police can take it away and destroy it.'

'But if they said "Yes",' went on Mr. Jenkins, 'then the police have no legal right to?'
'Then they are left entirely to their own devices. We wouldn't dream of taking it if they objected.'[1]

Which means that the police have no legal right to. Later the Metropolitan Police solicitor explained that when a magistrate found himself with a large number of publications and a letter saying that the owners were not defending them, he might say, 'Oh, well, if they don't object I won't look through all this stuff' (one such case involved 10,000 photographs) 'and I will not make an order. The police can deal with it by seeing the man and getting it destroyed.' The police felt they 'should be covered' in destroying it, so they invented the disclaimer form. The Yard's solicitor himself seemed not to like it much. It ought to disclaim possession rather than ownership, he thought: the man signing it might not be the owner. He might in effect be saying 'it doesn't belong to me – somebody else left it here,' perhaps to get himself out of trouble – or perhaps because it was true. 'We have never had such a case,' said the police solicitor, 'at any rate for 21 years.'[2] But whatever you may think of the 'disclaimer' procedure, it is at least a working system.

Twentieth-Century Trials

And it was all very much a twentieth-century procedure; justifiable (you might think) by the sheer bulk of the material involved, once you admit the case for control. But there was

1. *Ibid.* Q. 559.
2. *Ibid.* Q. 595.

no escape from Mr. Roy Jenkins's implication, and Mr.
Chuter Ede, another member, took it up. Among the trash
destroyed there *might* be a masterpiece? What kind of
policemen did this job? There were five of them in a Scotland
Yard 'obscenity squad'.

> 'In selecting five officers to form this squad,' Mr. Chuter
> Ede asked the Commissioner, 'do you pay any attention
> to their claims to be judges of literature and art?'
> 'None at all', was the disarming reply, 'we do not
> pretend that they are, any of them.'

They could be? Or if not, they could take someone with them
who was? It is tempting for anyone outside the beat genera-
tion, untouched by pop art, unexcited by those modern
cameramen who are waiting in the wings to take the 'L' out
of public, to sweep aside something meritorious among what
may seem obvious trash. I myself have seen photographic
exhibits at Old Bailey trials that could only move the
heart to pity and the mind to wonder at what the human
intellect has done to the single-minded simplicity of the
biological animal.

But there has lately appeared a disposition to call some of
these 'art', justifying this promotion by comparisons with
Rodin's *Bacchantes* or the ancient Indian or Mediterranean
sculptures. 'Self-evident pornography' may not be self-
evident after all; and the police, who are ordinary men, may
need a lot of fresh guidance. Lately the Courts have been
busily trying to supply this, groping their way towards a
'working definition' of obscenity.

Twentieth-Century Daring

As the publishers tiptoed into the twentieth century, it was
almost symbolical that its first year should see the publication,
side by side, of Freud's *Psychopathology of Everyday Life* and
Maeterlinck's *Life of the Bee*. In five more years the presses
had achieved a new pinnacle of daring with the publication
of Elinor Glyn's *Three Weeks*, which might never have
emerged from its deserved mediocrity but for its skilful
exploitation in America by Harry Reichenbach. Walter

Gelhorn tells the story in an essay called 'Restraints on Book Reading', published in 1960 by the American Library Association.[1] Gelhorn writes of D. H. Lawrence's insistence that 'subjects like venereal disease become dirty (and slyly cherished) only because of futile attempts to suppress mention of them.' In linguistics, he says:

> Words derive their deliciously vile connotations from restraints rather than from use. The late Harry Reichenbach, press agent extraordinary, put Lawrence's theory to practical commercial uses. He managed, by calling attention to a row of strategically placed asterisks, to persuade the Post Office Department to deny the mails to Elinor Glyn's *Three Weeks*. When the ban was lifted, as of course it eventually was, the demand for this shoddy novel moved it triumphantly to the best-seller lists.

Accordingly in England there was a furore about *Three Weeks*, which led to a vast expenditure of adolescent pocket-money and much angry disappointment. Neither the magistrates nor the criminal law judges ever had an opportunity to consider the corrupting qualities of *Three Weeks*, but in 1915 a motion picture company made a purposely and feebly ridiculous film of it. Elinor Glyn sued them for breach of copyright, and the obscenity question thus came before a High Court Judge as a non-criminal issue. Or if it didn't, Mr. Justice Younger was determined to proceed as if it had. What he said amounted to a decision that if a single judge, sitting in a Chancery court, took the view that a book was obscene, its author had no copyright in it:

> The episode described in the plaintiff's novel which she alleges has been pirated by the defendants, is in my opinion grossly immoral in its essence, its treatment and its tendency. Stripped of its trappings, which are mere accident,[2] it is nothing more or less than a sensual, adulterous intrigue. It is enough for me to say that to a book of such a cruelly destructive tendency no protection will be extended by a court of equity.

1. In *The First Freedom*. Edited by Robert B. Downs, 1960.
2. In *The Rainbow* and *Lady Chatterley* cases the accidental trappings were called padding (see p. 108).

Even harder now to believe, there was in the same year a prolonged uproar about H. G. Wells's utopian novel *In the Days of the Comet*, which was seen as a communistic attack on the sanctity of marriage. Almost with one voice the press gleefully attacked poor Wells and his 'poisonous' themes, to which he defiantly returned in *Ann Veronica*. There had been nothing erotically poisonous in his *Tono Bungay*, but its exposure of the current advertising and patent medicine rackets had not endeared him to the press. And then in the *New Machiavelli* (1911) he was being outrageous again about the rights and the inner feelings of women. If some of these and similar books were seized by the police and destroyed by order of magistrates, hardly anyone (as the law then stood) would know, certainly not Wells himself and probably not his publishers. There may well have been many such actions. Only occasionally did an important one come to light; and such was D. H. Lawrence's *The Rainbow*, published – and destroyed – in 1915, when you might have expected the first world war and the Defence of the Realm Act to be occupying the minds of the authorities to the exclusion of what the *literati* were reading.

The publishers were Methuen. On a complaint from a private citizen the police obtained a copy and took it to the Bow Street magistrate, Sir John Dickinson. No one will ever know whether he read it 'as a whole' or judged it by the erotic bits and dismissed the rest as 'padding'. But Sir John issued his warrant under the Obscene Publications Act 1857 (since replaced by similar provisions in the 1959 Act) for the seizure of all copies of *The Rainbow* to be found at Methuen's premises, the police came back with 1,000, and a summons was served upon Methuen's to 'show cause why the said books should not be destroyed'. The police solicitor said that the obscenity 'throughout' the book was

> wrapped up in language which I suppose will be regarded in some quarters as artistic and intellectual effort. I am at a loss, Sir, to understand how Messrs. Methuen came to lend their name to its publication.

Methuen's seemed to be at a loss too. They had twice asked Lawrence to modify it in manuscript, and the second time he had totally refused; so they decided (presumably after legal advice) to 'lend their name to it' as it stood then. All 1,000 copies were ordered to be destroyed. 'I am sorry', said the magistrate, 'that a firm of such high repute should have allowed their reputation to be soiled as it has been by the publication of this work.' There had been shocked criticism of the book in the popular press, of the all-too-familiar 'This Book Must be Banned' type; though the newly-proliferating weekly reviews treated it soberly. And the magistrate, who seemed to have been reading what the popular papers said, expressed the dangerous view that this alone should have induced the publishers to suppress it. (To savour the full danger of this proposition, you need merely to run through a list of the contemporary 'popular' critics. Make your own list.)

1915 was proving a successful year for the forces of censorship, and it may well be that more publishers' heads would have rolled if it had not been for that uncooperative victim Sir Stanley Unwin, whose head had stayed firmly in position throughout countless adventures. Allen & Unwin were now publishing Edward Carpenter's books, among which was *The Intermediate Sex* – published seven years earlier by a firm now defunct. One day in 1915 Sir Stanley had a visit from a policeman, who produced a copy of *The Intermediate Sex*, pointed out some marked passages, said that these had been the subject of a complaint and asked whether the book would accordingly be withdrawn. Sir Stanley assured him that it would not. Edward Carpenter, he told the officer, had just been praised throughout the country by literary men celebrating his birthday. Sir Stanley noticed that one 'objectionable' passage was doubly underlined, and he couldn't think why it was underlined at all. Later he was told at Scotland Yard that it had been completely misunderstood.[1] 'I deal with so much evil', said the mistaken officer, 'that I tend to see it where it doesn't exist.' And small wonder. Sir Stanley continued to publish the book, waiting stoically for the summons that never came. That was all right, but Sir Stanley's own comment shows what was all wrong:

1. *The Truth About Publishing.* Allen & Unwin, London, 7th ed, 1960, p. 315.

They were taking anonymous complaints much too seriously, and had succeeded with some publishers in getting books suppressed without anyone hearing about it. A great grievance, by the way, for the authors, who were surely entitled to be heard.

Well, if that still goes on today, there is nothing in the law to ensure that an author will hear any more about it than he would about a 'disclaimer' that sent his book to the furnace without trial.[2]

Frank Harris's *My Life and Loves*, published in France (but printed in English) in 1922, now began to appear in plain wrappers in the Paris bookshops, and to be seized by British customs officers on its intended way into British households. It also got into the Soho bookshops; and many a copy of it was destroyed, with other less pretentious erotica, by magisterial order or by virtue of 'disclaimers' signed by prudent booksellers. But if it has ever been the subject of a prosecution in this country, there seem to be no reports of it. Today, the corruptible can buy it in cheap paperback and it has, accordingly, disappeared from the 'Rare Books' columns of the small advertisement pages. But also in 1922, and also in Paris, there appeared the long-awaited *Ulysses* of James Joyce. It, too, was smuggled in single copies into England; and it seems that whenever it was seized by Customs Officers, the deprived smuggler always accepted his deprivation. I am indebted to a retired Customs Officer for the information that his own enquiries, addressed (as opportunity seemed to offer) to reasonably friendly smugglers, had established three common reasons for this docility. First, the smuggler had been trying to read the book on the plane or boat coming over, had given it up in perplexity, and wished he hadn't paid all that money for it. Second, he didn't want to challenge the Customs decision in open Court and get his name into the papers. Third, the words in the book were so startling in print that you could never hope to win.

Nevertheless, the smuggling went on until 1936, when The Bodley Head brought out the present edition, which

2. See p. 66-67.

has been four times reprinted and never (in Britain) prosecuted. And by 1936, as I have mentioned earlier, it was
possible for it to contain as an appendix the famous Woolsey
judgment in the Federal Court in New York. The events
leading up to that judgment will bear re-examination.

The 'Ulysses' Judgment

Countless copies had been burned in the United States,
mainly by postal and customs authorities. The more copies
they burned, the more people saw it as a status-symbol to
own one. You could furtively take it out and show people;
you didn't have to try reading it. Copies changed hands at
upwards of 200 dollars each, and it is said that a *Ulysses* black
market was being run by men whose normal vocabulary
was almost confined to the four-letter words that had got it
such a bad name. This went on for twelve years, until
Random House had a copy sent over from France, alerted
the Customs men, and prepared for the fray. The cheapest
and least dangerous way to get a judgment on a book, in
America as in Great Britain, is the one that only Random
House seem ever to have exploited; namely, to pay someone
to bring it through the Customs shed, get it impounded,
challenge the act of impounding it, and let the Customs men
try to prove their charge of obscenity. You can do this in
England even with a book published in England, taking it
abroad and then bringing it ostentatiously back with you.

Something usually goes wrong in these staged offences,
and this time it was the Customs network that failed. The
book got through undetected and the addressee had to take
it back and remind the Customs men of their duty. Thus
Ulysses was at last before a Court, on the ground that its
importation was in breach of the Tariff Act of 1930. This was
partly because of its four-letter words and partly because its
portrayal of the two-level thought-process had been presented
by Joyce with unaccustomed frankness. Incidentally, there
were Joyce enthusiasts who went on as though he was the
first writer ever to have realised that a man can, simul-
taneously, reflect that providence is inscrutable and that he
wants to go to the lavatory. Joyce breaks new ground in his

use of those economical expressions for the lower half of the thought-stream to which they were more appropriate. Judge Woolsey likened the result to a doubly-exposed photographic negative. He took a great interest in them and in the genteel-isms that do the same job when the police are listening. He asked defending counsel what was the genteelism for coitus. 'Oh, "they slept together", your honour – it means the same thing.' The Judge grinned. 'But does it?' he said. 'That isn't even usually the truth.' When he wanted to know whether Counsel had really read the entire book, the defence attorney (who had) began to fear its suppression on the ground that no one would be hurt by not being allowed to read the unreadable. 'Tough going, isn't it?' said Judge Woolsey. But then he disclosed how, since he was sitting without a jury, he had done what every juror in a British Court is warned that he simply *must not* do.

'Do not discuss this book with anyone, members of the jury,' our Judges say. 'Remember that you alone are to decide on its alleged obscenity and on whatever other qualities it may have. Keep your own counsel.' It always sounds right and reasonable. But when Judge Woolsey had made up his mind about *Ulysses,* or (as he would be more likely to say) thought he had, he took this extraordinary course and openly announced the result. He had already stated his famous principle about the need, in these cases, for some such arbiter as 'the reasonable man' in the law of tort and 'the man learned in the art' in the law of patents. He thought one should postulate 'a man with average sex instincts' or, as the French call him, *l'homme moyen sensuel.* And then:

I checked my impression with two friends of mine who, in my opinion, answered to the above-stated requirement. These literary assessors, as I might properly describe them, were called on separately; neither knew that I was consulting the other. They are men whose opinions on literature and on life I value most highly. They both read *Ulysses* and, of course, were wholly uncon-nected with this case. Without letting either of my assessors know what my decision was, I gave to each of them the legal definition of obscene and asked each whether in his opinion *Ulysses* was obscene within that definition. I was interested to find that they both agreed with my opinion: that reading *Ulysses* in its entirety, as a book must be read on such a test as this, did not tend to excite sexual impulses or lustful thoughts but that its net effect on them was only that of a somewhat tragic and very powerful commentary on the inner lives of men and women. It is only with the normal person that the law is concerned. Such a test as I have described therefore is the only proper test of obscenity in the case of a book like *Ulysses*, which is a sincere and serious attempt to devise a new literary method for the observation and description of mankind.

The prosecution appealed to the Circuit Court of Appeals, whose judges were duly appraised of Woolsey's recourse to what he must have thought was the American equivalent of 'The man on the Clapham omnibus'. The Appeal Judges took no objection. They made no suggestion that an 'assessor' whose opinion would be 'highly valued' by Judge Woolsey would not be a 'normal person' and would seldom be found on any kind of omnibus. They delivered judgments, two in favour of *Ulysses* and one against, that are not less impressive than Judge Woolsey's. And the government took the case no further: the Supreme Court of the United States has never had to pronounce upon *Ulysses*. The day when it was given such an opportunity would quite probably mark the arrival of a new puritan revolution; for *Ulysses*, rather than any other book that the Judges have had to read in the present century, represented a publishing climacteric. 'If the government fails over this book,' wrote a New York District Attorney at the time[1], 'that's the end. That's as far as we go. I guess I know what's obscene, and you do, and the man on the corner, and my wife and your wife, and his wife. The Judge will say it's what our kind of person thinks that goes. But it is not. It's what that Judge is going to think.'

As this book goes to press, the Director of Public Prosecutions has under consideration a reduced (but by no means expurgated) edition of the long-outlawed book by Walter

1. Personal letter to the author.

called *My Secret Life*; and it is currently being said in prosecuting circles that 'if this book is acquitted, we're beaten'. But *courage, mes braves:* it would only be a lost battle. The war will always go on.

Radclyffe Hall or Prussic Acid

In England the oft-told tale of *The Well of Loneliness* grows even less credible with each telling. It must here be noted in rather more detail than on previous pages, for it involved a magisterial decision, and still more a tactical error on the part of the defence, that may have affected the course of events for the next 25 years. Let us look first, with all due honour to the remarkable legal man responsible for it, at what is now regarded among lawyers as a major procedural blunder.

The Well of Loneliness is a moving story of ecstatic and unhappy love between women. Its author, Miss Radclyffe Hall, can be said to have been in the Marie Corelli, Ethel M. Dell and Ruby M. Ayres tradition, known at the time as 'Came the Dawn'. Far from depraving or corrupting anyone, her book could only have brought a kind of sad and lonely comfort to women readers similarly victimised by society and by a pathological condition as natural as it is timeless. It was published in 1928 by Jonathan Cape, received by the *Times Literary Supplement* as 'sincere, courageous, high-minded and often beautifully expressed', and praised by most of the leading contemporary reviewers including Arnold Bennett ('honest, convincing, extremely courageous'). Its tenderness was apparent, one would have thought, to all. Then suddenly, amid this chorus of praise, the voice of the egregious James Douglas of the *Sunday Express* was heard in the land:

> This novel forces upon our Society a disagreeable task which it has hitherto shirked, the task of cleaning itself from the leprosy of these lepers and making the air clean and wholesome once more. . . . It flings a veil of sentiment over their depravity. It even suggests that their self-made debasement is unavoidable because they cannot save themselves. . . . I would rather put a phial of prussic acid in the hands of a healthy girl or boy than the book in question.

Unlike James Douglas and his paper, the *Sunday Chronicle* rather made a business of ferreting out 'vice' as a perennial lucrative quarry. So it, too, condemned *The Well of Loneliness* and did it rather excitingly. One or two fringe papers joined in. And it must have seemed to the publishers that the path of wisdom would be to prod the ground a little before going further. They wrote to the Home Secretary and asked him to prod it for them.

It would be useless to do this today. It is true that until 1946 the Home Office considered itself to be involved in such matters; and, though it was never a publishers' advice bureau, it gave many an indication that it would not be likely to initiate any action against a particular book, adding that there would still be nothing to stop some private individual or society from doing so. More importantly, it often indicated that prosecution *would* be likely, though this took the form of a 'suggestion' that the book might be perhaps 'withdrawn from circulation'. Until the making of the Prosecution of Offences Regulations, 1946, and their involvement of the Director of Public Prosecutions, it was not unusual for the Home Secretary to *direct* the D.P.P. to prosecute. (This is no longer possible, though he might send the D.P.P. a book that someone had sent to him, a gesture surely not without some meaning.) The dangers were obvious. A Home Secretary could stop publication of a book that the Courts might think innocuous. This is what happened, in the first instance, about *The Well of Loneliness*. The Home Secretary was Sir William Joynson-Hicks, later Lord Brentford, Tory M.P. for Twickenham, a leading Evangelical and president of the National Church League. (He was largely responsible for the defeat of the Alternative Prayer Book measure in 1928 – the year of *The Well of Loneliness*.) During the Select Committee's enquiries in 1957, Mr. Kenneth Robinson, M.P., asked Sir Frank Newsam, Home Office Under-Secretary, a pertinent question about him:

Is it unreasonable to assume, as so many people do, that the tenure of office of Sir William Joynson-Hicks was responsible for rigid applications of the law with regard to obscene publications, or was it purely fortuitous that there were a number of prosecutions during his tenure of office?

Since 1946 (replied Sir Frank Newsam) the Home Office has had nothing to do with prosecutions. Before 1946 it was open to the Secretary of State to direct the D.P.P. to prosecute. I don't know whether Sir William Joynson-Hicks took a particular interest in these matters or not.[1]

A good many other people knew. But it is fair to Joynson-Hicks to say that Jonathan Cape's letter *offered to withdraw the book* – and that Miss Radclyffe Hall, who had not been consulted, was furious about it. If someone publishes a book that sparks off a tremendous row, and the immunity of it is obviously going to be one more stick with which the Press can belabour the most beaten-up of all Ministerial departments, what does a Home Secretary do when the publisher asks him if he would like the book withdrawn? That was what Joynson-Hicks did. Naturally enough this was seen as a new and sinister form of censorship and was widely attacked accordingly; and the attacks may have encouraged Cape's to connive with The Pegasus Press in Paris to bring out another edition ('in which not one word has been altered'), and to circularise possible English readers that it was available, after all, by post. Not surprisingly, the first consignment of this edition was seized by Customs men at Dover and an application was promptly made to the Bow Street magistrate for the destruction of all the books seized.

Norman Birkett, K.C., was there on the publisher's behalf (with Herbert Metcalfe, who later became a Metropolitan Magistrate himself), 'to show cause why the said books should not be destroyed'. Miss Radclyffe-Hall was there too, though (as the law then stood) she had no right to be heard and could only be an outraged spectator. She made one angry effort to interrupt and was told she would be ejected if she did it again.

The magistrate was Sir Chartres Biron, who was by way of being a literary man himself and reviewed in *The Observer* a range of books by no means confined to the law – the one subject, it was uncharitably said by lawyers, that he knew least about.

---

1. *Minutes of Evidence Taken before the Select Committee on the Obscene Publications Bill*, No. 122 of 1956/7. Q. 47.

The trial got off to what should have been a bad start because Mr. Eustace Fulton, for the Crown, asked the police officer whether *he* thought the book was obscene – the one inadmissible question, the one consideration that *must* be left to magistrate or jury alone. But the magistrate seemed not to think of disallowing the question when addressed to a policeman. The policeman weighed in. Oh yes, he thought it was: and offensive, because it dealt with physical passion(!). It was also indecent 'because it deals with an indecent subject'. The police were very sensitive in those days.

Mr. Birkett announced, in pursuance of the principle commended by Sir James FitzJames Stephen 70 years before,[1] that he was proposing to call 'evidence from every conceivable walk of life which bears on the test whether the tendency of this book is to deprave and corrupt'. He added that a more distinguished body of witnesses had never before been called in a Court of Justice. Sir Chartres Biron said he doubted whether their evidence could be admitted, and Birkett retorted that if it couldn't a magistrate was a censor of literature. Biron, who probably thought he was, said that witnesses could not be allowed to express their opinions upon matters which were for the decision of the court; having, presumably, forgotten what the police witness had been allowed to say. Nevertheless, Birkett went ahead and called for Mr. Desmond MacCarthy.

Are you the editor of *Life and Letters*?
I am.
Have you read this book?
Yes.
In your view is it obscene?

But this was different. What a police officer thought, perhaps, didn't matter much, but Desmond MacCarthy – Eton, Trinity, Leipzig, literary editor and dramatic critic of the *New Statesman* – this was the Hazlitt of his time. The magistrate wasn't proposing to listen to him. A book might be a fine piece of literature, he said, and yet obscene. Art and obscenity were not at all dissociated. 'It does not follow that because a book is a work of art it is not obscene. I shall

1. See p. 27.

not admit the evidence.' (Another twenty years were to elapse before the higher courts conceded that a book could be both artistic *and* obscene, and that the former quality *might* be more socially important than the latter.) Birkett formally tendered 39 other witnesses; and the magistrate said that, although he was delighted to hear that all these literary ladies and gentlemen were in attendance, he could decide without their aid whether *The Well of Loneliness* was an obscene book. So he decided it was and they all went home.

FitzJames Stephen must have been revolving in his grave. Let us remind ourselves of what the great law-giver had said in 1877:

> A person is justified in publishing . . . obscene books . . . for the public good, as being necessary or advantageous to religion or morality, to the administration of justice, the pursuit of science, literature or art, or other objects of general interest.

Birkett's question to Desmond MacCarthy, by common subsequent consent or hindsight, should have been not 'Is this book obscene?' but 'Whether this book is obscene or not – and that of course is a matter for the learned magistrate – is its publication advantageous to the pursuit of literature?' If *that* question had been disallowed, and all the *literati* present to answer it had been sent away unheard, there would have been a powerful ground of appeal (preferably not to Quarter Sessions, but to the High Court on a point of law). 'Expert evidence' might then have been declared admissible, and some of the more ridiculous prosecutions of the next 30 years would have been avoided. As it was, an appeal to the County of London Sessions (at which Birkett did *not* appear) was predictably and expensively futile. But the book was republished in 1949 without fuss, and at the moment of writing a paperback is in preparation.

'Sleeveless Errand'

The Home Secretary came in for much abuse, though all he had done (he could claim) was to agree with the somewhat masochistic suggestion of Jonathan Cape's that *The Well of*

Loneliness ought to be 'withdrawn'. (Cape's implication, of course, had been: 'Leave us alone and we'll cut our losses.' And the losses must have been considerable, to say nothing of the hurt to the feeling of the defenceless author.) But within a few months, another book had been sent to Joynson Hicks with a letter of complaint, and he was in the news again as 'Jix' the puritanical purge of publishing. This time it was a novel by Norah James called *Sleeveless Errand*, consisting mainly of a Joycean-type dialogue between a couple expressing themselves with a total lack of restraint on matters where restraint had, so far, been more usual. Jix sent it to the D.P.P. The D.P.P. asked the Bow Street Magistrate (this time Mr. Rollo Graham Campbell) for a destruction order, and the magistrate, granting it, rejected the publisher's argument that the author's purpose had been to 'portray *and condemn* the mode of life and language of a certain section of the community'. What it condemned was adultery. This was the beginning, and not an auspicious one, of a period in which allegedly 'obscene' books were to be defended on the ground that they condemned the obscenity that they portrayed. But 'I can't accept the view,' Mr. Graham Campbell said, 'that the book in its result is not obscene if the passages referred to are not held up to glorification.'

Which was fair enough. Yet that was to be the burden of many a defence from this time forward. And that, indeed, was what now began to distinguish the defence of obscenity from the defence of pornography; that the former condemned what it portrayed while the latter did not condemn at all – the sponsors of the latter, when put to it, claimed at the most that it was cathartic and at the least that it really did no harm. *Sleeveless Errand* went to the flames.

Lawrence's Poems

Then in 1929 the Postmaster General, acting under the powers given to him by the Post Office Act of 1908, intercepted in the mails a group of D. H. Lawrence poems collected under the name of *Pansies*, on their way to the publishers, Martin Secker Ltd. They were in manuscript form and (Jix told some angry questioners in the House of Commons) had been mailed as 'open book post', which was sometimes 'investigated' as a matter of G.P.O. routine. The Post Office was disturbed by them and sent them to the Home Office – today, if a postal official could bring himself to think them indecent, they would go straight to the Director of Public Prosecutions. The Home Office agreed about their indecency and thus they reached the D.P.P. by the more roundabout route. He suggested to the publishers that some of the poems should be scrapped, and they were. *Pansies*, 1929, is not the same book as *Pansies*, 1928. It was never suggested that these poems were 'obscene'. The postmen found them 'indecent'. The Post Office Act penalises anyone who encloses in a postal packet

> any *indecent or obscene* print, painting, photograph, litho-graph, cinematograph film, book, card or written communication, or any *indecent or obscene* article whether similar to the above or not.

And although an obscene article is almost certainly indecent, as the High Court said in 1965,[1] an indecent article is not necessarily obscene. At that time the word indecent meant what any judge or magistrate took it to mean.

And Lawrence's Pictures

Six months later they took it to mean pubic hair, which is visible in the work of a thousand artists but was intolerable in Lawrence's paintings, because he also wrote non-reticent novels and poems. Pubic hair in a Modigliani or a Matisse might be just about tolerable, because they made no pretence to be anything other than artists, and you knew what those people were like. Lawrence was a novelist and poet, and a reprehensible one, only pretending to be an artist. When the Warren Galleries in London put on an exhibition of his paintings in July 1929 it was raided by the police, solely because of the hair. There has always been speculation about the means by which Mr. Frederick Mead, the Great Marlborough Street Magistrate, was convinced under the law as it then stood (the Obscene Publications Act,

1. *R.* v. *Stanley*, 1965, 1 All E.R. 1035.

1857) that there were pictures at the Warren Galleries that ought to be destroyed, and that he must arm the police with the necessary warrant to bring them before him. Did he go along to the Galleries to have a look? Did the police just swear by Almighty God that they had seen what they thought was hair? A popular view at the time was that they merely had to depose that the pictures were the work of this Lawrence fellow. The paintings were seized and the lessees of the Warren Galleries were summoned to show cause why they should not go to the flames.

For the defence, Mr. St. John Hutchinson urged (without much conviction, according to those who heard him) that they were works of art. Some notable artists and critics were there to say the same thing, including Sir William Orpen, Augustus John and Sir William Rothenstein. The magistrate waved them away as Sir Chartres Biron had waved away Mr. Desmond MacCarthy and the others, but with far less justification. They were not there to say that the paintings were not obscene. Their evidence was to be that, obscene or not, they were artistic – they 'furthered the interests of art'. Even as the law then stood, it is probable that the magistrate ought to have heard them. St. John Hutchinson knew this and was prepared to accept judgment for the moment and take the case to the High Court. But this can be expensive even if you win. The Judges have a way of 'making no order as to costs', which means that, even as the victor, you pay everything out of your own pocket, and, in particular, they will take this course where they don't much like the look, taste or smell of the appeal and the appellant. Who could say how they would react to the hair? And here was Mr. Frederick Mead offering to dismiss the summons on payment of a mere five guineas costs if the Lawrence exhibition was closed. Hutchinson took the offer and, to Lawrence's lifelong mortification, the exhibition was closed.

'Surprising Songs'

In 1932 there occurred what is probably the most extraordinary 'obscenity' trial of the century, the tragi-comedy of Count Geoffrey Wladislas Vaile Potocki de Montalk, poet, playwright, eccentric and (he always said) uncrowned King of Poland. He was a familiar figure in the Soho of the 'thirties, and his dress out-Carnabied the Soho of the 'sixties – a wine-coloured cloak that swept the ground, bare feet in leather sandals, hair falling about his shoulders. (Whenever I saw him, which was quite often, he had an unaccountable retinue of pretty girls.) He owned and edited an odd little paper called *The Right Review*, in which he published his own verses and pursued his claim to the Polish throne. He had published one or two books of verse (one of them was called *Surprising Songs*), and their quality was deemed sufficient to establish him as an occasional reviewer of poetry for *The Observer*. Then he put together some translated poems of Rabelais and a parody of Verlaine, 'coarse' enough to frighten off any English publisher, and looked around for a printer who would enable him to publish them 'privately'.

He found an apparently willing linotype man and left the manuscript with him. The printer found that they contained words usually employed only by the less restrained scribblers on public walls. And he took them to the police. The police took legal advice, and Count de Montalk was summoned before the Bow Street magistrate on a Common Law charge of 'publishing an obscene libel'.

Why? If the police thought that Verlaine and Rabelais must be kept out of susceptible reach, why not ask simply for a destruction order? But de Montalk was committed for trial at the Old Bailey, and the Magistrate would not allow him bail in his own recognizances: he must find a surety. An incredible decision, since de Montalk had a known address and was highly unlikely to run away. He had been trained for the law, loved a battle, and was here engaged in one after his own heart. But he had to spend three days in the remand wing of Brixton Prison before his brother was able to find the necessary sureties. He was then released on bail.

On the 8th February, 1932, the trial came on before the Recorder of London, Sir Ernest Wild, K.C. The defendant was still wearing his long wine-coloured cloak,[1] and the Recorder contemplated him with obvious distaste. He was

1. I happened to be in Court throughout this trial. – C.H.R.

very ably defended by Mr C. G. L. du Cann, himself a writer of distinction; and the Recorder reminded him of his good fortune in this regard, allowing it to be understood that he himself was also a writer of poems. (In fact he had published, the year before, a volume of verses of an almost unbelievable banality called *The Lamp of Destiny*.) The jury read the de Montalk poems, police and other witnesses told how they had come to official notice, and Mr. du Cann called his client to the witness-box to give evidence on his own behalf. There de Montalk brushed aside the proffered Testament when he was asked to take the oath: his religion was paganism.

'Do you wish to affirm?' the Recorder asked him coldly.

He did not. He would swear in his own way.

'You will either take the oath or you will take an affirmation.'

He would do neither. He would swear, he said, by Apollo. There was a shocked silence, followed by a brief discussion as to the propriety of allowing pagan oaths in Christian courts. Finally the Recorder decided to let him swear by Apollo and see how it went. Montalk raised both arms above his head and the wine-coloured cloak hung from them like threatening wings. No one heard what he said, which may have been just as well.

'Do you now consider yourself sworn to speak the truth?' asked the Recorder, who had really been rather patient.

He did. His evidence proceeded, the Recorder taking it upon himself to do quite a lot of the cross-examining.

'Members of the jury', he said, when it came to the summing-up, 'you are men of the world. You know what these words mean?' He indicated them by their initial letters only. 'We all know what they mean? Are you going to allow a man, just because he calls himself a poet, to deflower our English language by popularising these words? ... A man must not say he is a poet and be filthy. He has to obey the law just the same as ordinary citizens, and the sooner the highbrow school learns that, the better for the morality of the country.'[1]

1. Alec Craig, *The Banned Books of England and Other Countries*. Allen & Unwin, London, 1962.

Perhaps the most extraordinary word in this summing-up was 'popularising'. Is that what the poet was doing with these old, universally-known four-letter words? And should they rather be kept from the people? The learned Recorder may have been right, since they have now become the *sine qua non* of the more recherché novel, and experiments are taking place which, it is hoped, may replace them as swearwords for the proletariat. The jury returned their verdict of Guilty and the indignant Recorder passed the incredible sentence of six months' imprisonment. Judge and jury between them, believe it or not, had decided:

(1) that the famous monosyllables, known to every citizen over the age of five, could corrupt and deprave someone reading them in a book,

(2) that the law had therefore been broken merely by showing them to a printer, since this was 'publication', and

(3) that the man who showed them to another man must go to prison as a criminal.

De Montalk's case was taken to the Court of Criminal Appeal whose judges had to consider it in the full knowledge that it was being paid for by literary men as eminent as T. S. Eliot, Lord Esher, Laurence Housman, Aldous Huxley, Walter de la Mare, J. B. Priestley, Hugh Walpole and H. G. Wells. Those giants were not saying, and had not been asked to say, that Montalk's poems were good. Their concern was the same as Milton's; it was indignant; and they paid up generously.

But the stupefying fact is that, as recently as 1932, the Appeal Court Judges could uphold not merely such a conviction but such a sentence. De Montalk served his time in Wormwood Scrubs Prison, and came out to describe his experiences in a pamphlet called *Snobbery With Violence*. Nevertheless, Mr. du Cann had made the case legally memorable by getting FitzJames Stephen's proposition admitted into the Common Law of England[1]:

That it is a good defence to the charge of publishing an obscene libel that the publication of matter *prima facie*

1. See p. 27.

obscene was for the public good, as being necessary or advantageous to religion, science, literature or art, provided that the manner and extent of the publication do not exceed what the public interest requires.

The Beginnings of 'Expert' Evidence

There still had not emerged the pattern of procedure for which the law seemed designed: 'destruction order' summonses where the books were obviously without pretensions to literary merit, prosecution – with the right to jury trial – where there was something to be said for them. In 1935 there were three representative cases of note – two were prosecutions and one was not. Boriswoode's Ltd. were fined £250 (and two directors £50 each) at Manchester Assizes for publishing James Hanley's *Boy*: and Heinemann's pleaded guilty before the Bow Street Magistrate when accused of obscenity in publishing the novel *Bessie Cotter* by Wallace Smith – they had to pay £100 and 100 guineas costs. On the other hand Edward Charles's well-known manual of sex instruction *The Sex Impulse*, whose publishers were the unfortunate Boriswoode Ltd. again, was selected for a 'destruction order' summons. It reflected the influence of de Montalk's case in that the Magistrate allowed the evidence of experts for the defence. But it was hardly a major breakthrough; for, having listened to it, he brushed it all aside as irrelevant to what he had to consider.

They were, moreover, educational, medical and scientific experts. The idea that there could be literary experts had not yet really taken root. The publishers had submitted the manuscript to a distinguished physician, Dr. Jeneen of the Westminster Hospital, whose report commended it to them; and they sent the galley-proofs, with similarly encouraging results, to Sir Julian Huxley (who in due course wrote an Introduction to the book), to Lord Horder, to Dr. Janet Chance, and to Dr. Voge of the medical faculty at Edinburgh University.

At the hearing before Mr. Ronald Powell, the Metropolitan Magistrate at Westminster, expert evidence about the book's educational and scientific value was given by

Professor Malinowski (who was then probably the foremost living social anthropologist), Professor J. B. S. Haldane, Professor Julian Huxley, Dr. Janet Chance, and Miss Maude Royden. In dismissing their evidence as valueless, the Magistrate made a statement of the law that must now seem extraordinary to those who have followed its development:

> I have not to decide whether this book is of any medical or psychological value. The only thing for me to decide is whether it comes under the heading of an obscene book.

And it was obscene, he said. So he ordered its destruction; and the publishers appealed – not to the High Court, where they could perhaps have got a decision on the magistrate's unexpected ruling, but to the County of London Sessions. An appeal to Quarter Sessions is in effect a complete retrial. It simply treads the same old ground, all the witnesses being called again; and all the experts were duly called. Again they were ignored. The book was obscene, said the Chairman of the Appeals Committee, and off to the flames it went.

What were the experts for? It has been surmised that in *The Sexual Impulse* case they were defending a book that committed the cardinal error of taking sex lightly or (worse) happily. Levity is a difficult thing to defend in a court of law, and the witnesses named were perhaps rather a solemn-looking lot who would find it specially incongruous. The law had taken a minute step forward, but things didn't feel much different.

'Threats' of Proceedings

No publisher knew what course the Crown might adopt in taking a book to Court. Many a book was scrapped after the police had called to say that there were complaints about it and that 'proceedings' might be taken: they seldom seemed to know what kind of proceedings. In 1938 Routledge published an autobiography in one part of which the authoress, pseudonymously called Sheila Cousins, described her life as a prostitute. It was called *To Beg I am Ashamed*. The Public Morality Council sent a copy to the Home Secretary, Sir Samuel Hoare (later Lord Templewood). He, as was now usual but not yet obligatory, sent it to the D.P.P.; and two police officers called at Routledge's to say that there would be 'serious consequences' if the book were not withdrawn. Review copies had gone out – and had wrung protests from the *Daily Mail*, the *Daily Mirror* and the *Spectator*. The publishers withdrew it; sixteen years later it was republished without objection from anyone.

The 'Corruption' Test

By this time there had developed, as there was bound to develop sooner or later, a 'chain of causation' in deciding whether a book was to be prosecuted. It worked rather like this, as explained to the Select Committee in 1958 by Sir Frank Newsam, Home Office Under-Secretary of State. The Chairman, Sir Patrick Spens, was asking him what the Home Office did when it received a book alleged to be obscene.

'We don't prosecute or express an opinion on it,' said Sir Frank Newsam. 'If we think the thing wants looking at, then we refer it to the Director of Public Prosecutions, and thereafter we cease to have any further duty in the matter.'

'Would it be fair to say that you do in fact exercise a degree of censorship yourselves inside the Home Office?'

'I should think it would be most unfair to say that – unless the case is so absurd that we won't even bother the Director of Public Prosecutions with it.'

And he instanced the supposedly Romano-British hillside Giant of Cerne Abbas, in Dorset (a figure cut out of the grass and down to the chalk), whose shameless anatomical details had moved some embarrassed citizens who had just noticed them to seek Home Office protection. They wanted a bit more grass grown. The Home Office just laughed and laughed, said Sir Frank Newsam. Lord Lambton took up the questioning.

'What is your idea', he asked, 'of a recommendation to the D.P.P.?'

'We make no recommendation to him.'

'The D.P.P. says in his Memorandum that 49 cases were received from the Home Office?'

'Not with a recommendation, but for consideration.'

'Without any comment?'

'Without comment.'

'But surely the act of sending them to him is tacitly a recommendation for prosecution in itself?'

'I don't agree with you. We don't make any recommendation or any suggestion for prosecution. And if the thing is palpable nonsense, then we don't even bother the D.P.P. with it at all.'

Back to the drawing-board. Surely (said Lord Lambton) the fact that the Home Office *selected* certain cases—

They are almost all cases where the Post Office find the stuff and report it to us and we refer it to the D.P.P., unless it's so silly that we don't bother about it. We wouldn't want you to think that the D.P.P. takes no notice of the Home Office, but the fact that it comes from the Home Office is no indication that we think it is a case for prosecution – none whatever.

Can you believe that? Actually Lord Lambton gave it up. But it can now be revealed (as all journalists love to say) that the buck has been followed to its final resting place, probably the most agile buck in all the corridors of power. No one will admit to exercising any judgment, passing any opinion, having any feelings. But at last the Committee got to the Director of Public Prosecutions, Sir Theobald Matthews; and he was asked about 'final responsibility' by Mr. Elwyn Jones.[1] Sir Theobald had put in a Memorandum that contained this paragraph:

As Director of Public Prosecutions I should strongly deprecate my Department being placed in the position, which apparently it is thought by some persons to occupy already, of being a literary or moral censor.

Mr. Elwyn Jones referred back to this. 'On the whole,' he said, 'when in doubt, you err on the side of prosecution? Is that right?'

'I think I actually cover myself, if there is any doubt about it,' replied the D.P.P., 'in practically every case by putting it before Treasury Counsel for advice. I am always

1. Now Sir Elwyn Jones, Q.C., H.M. Attorney-General.

preaching to my Department, and to myself, that we are *not* the people who decide whether something is obscene or not. That is a matter for the courts.'

'If Treasury Counsel advise one way or the other, do you generally act in the way Treasury Counsel advise?'

'Certainly. That is my protection.'

No one asked what was Treasury Counsel's protection, out there at the end of the line. No one seemed surprised that the D.P.P., for example, should defer (as he did and still does) to another lawyer who was in fact his junior – Treasury Counsel at the Old Bailey. If you ask any holder of that office what standards he applies in saying yea or nay to a 'dirty book' prosecution, you will at last be talking to the man who cannot disclaim any powers of censorship, who cannot, as everyone else does, 'strongly deprecate being placed in that position'. He is the *Ultima Thule*. I have had the temerarious experience, as an impudent journalist, of asking one such man what it was that would make him decide on a prosecution as he read a book, or as he closed a finished book and sat thinking. I would not disclose his name on the rack, for he told me (after much importunate questioning most good-humouredly borne) that the test was whether he felt randy. 'Entirely subjective', he said, 'but what else is there? The subjective has got to come into it at *some* point. All very well for these people to say they aren't censors, as though that was something poisonous. And all very well for them to go around talking about the "objective test". When it comes to the crunch there's only me, and how I feel myself reacting.'

I saw what he meant, and pondered it. In terms of the future of English literature, it was a solemn thought, though one realised that there *might* be kinds of 'obscenity' that had to do with violence, cruelty, or drug addiction, none of which would produce amatory tinglings in a Senior Treasury Counsel at the Old Bailey. We will be coming to them later.

The Attorney-General's Part

But he was not *really* alone. Mr. Elwyn-Jones, soon to be Attorney-General himself, wanted to know whether the Attorney-General came into all this.

'He could', said Sir Theobald Matthew, 'as being first of all the person under whose general direction I act; and secondly, as the senior of all Treasury Counsel, so to speak, to whom I have occasion to refer. I think I have twice, since I have been Director, worried the Attorney-General about books.'

'I seem to remember one occasion some years ago?'

'*The Naked and the Dead?*'

'Yes', said Mr. Elwyn Jones, who had probably been reading all this up. And later the D.P.P. was asked more about it by Mr. J. E .S. Simon, Q.C.,[1] who reminded him that *The Naked and the Dead* had been the subject of a series of Parliamentary questions.

'The *Sunday Times*', said the D.P.P., 'had said that it was an obscene work which ought to be prosecuted.'

'Not the *Sunday Express*?'

'No, it was the *Sunday Times* on this occasion.'

'Was it prosecuted?'

'No.'

But what the D.P.P. did *not* say was that the publishers, Alan Wingate Ltd., were advised to withdraw the book after the *Sunday Times*'s entertaining onslaught, and refused. 'It is our moral and literary duty to publish it,' they said in a published statement. 'It presents a true picture of the way soldiers talked and behaved during the war, and American reviewers have compared it with Stendhal and Tolstoy.' (You would find, on comparison, that Stendhal and Tolstoy presented their pictures of military men in more muted language.)

Also what the D.P.P. did *not* say was that the Attorney-General at the time, Sir Hartley Shawcross, Q.C.,[2] had answered the Parliamentary questions thus:[3]

In cases of the kind involved here there are two public interests to which I must have regard. It is important that no publisher should be permitted to deprave or corrupt morals, to exalt vice, or to encourage its commission. It is also important that there should be the least

1. Now Sir Jocelyn Simon, President of the Probate, Divorce and Admiralty Division of the High Court.

2. Now Lord Shawcross.

3. *Hansard*, 23rd May, 1949.

possible interference with the freedom of publication and that the Attorney-General should not seek to make the criminal law a vehicle for imposing a censorship on the frank discussion or portrayal of sordid and unedifying aspects of life simply on the grounds of offence against taste or manners. While there is much in this most tedious and lengthy book which is foul, lewd and revolting, looking at it as a whole I do not think that its *intent* is to corrupt or deprave, or that it is likely to lead to any other result than disgust at its contents.

So *The Naked and the Dead* was profitably stigmatised without having to come before the Courts. But, much more significantly, here was a Law Officer talking as though the *intent* of the author and publisher had once again become legally important. He turned out to be right, but the importance was short-lived.

The 1954 'Purge'

We are approaching the 1954 prosecutions that changed the law, the 'purge' that alarmed the literary world and convinced everyone that books must be rescued from the Common Law and the Judges, and protected once for all (perennial pipe-dream of the law reformer) by way of a clearly-expressed Act of Parliament. In the previous year there had been an Interpol Conference at Oslo, and the suppression of obscene literature was on its agenda. Interpol[1] is not, as some TV pupils suppose, an international corps of tight-lipped Bonds patrolling the world in Bentleys, hovercraft and bullet-proof pullovers, and tackling criminals too powerful and dangerous for slow-moving national police forces. It's a system of communication, with a small secretariat in Paris and an aptitude for arranging conferences in surroundings of splendid scenery. On its 1953 agenda was the apparent ineffectiveness of the current Convention for the Suppression of the Traffic in Obscene Literature. The Conference concluded that among the causes of crime, particularly sexual offences, was the reading of pornography;

1. The International Criminal Police Commission. For the best account of this, see Sir Richard Jackson, *Occupied With Crime*. Harrap, London, 1966.

and its numerous delegates went back home with a new
resolve. Before we consider its immediate consequences, and
by way of examining a rather new link in the chain of
prosecution, here comes a brief digression on the effect of
reading upon crime. Not a pronouncement: no one knows,
not even the Kinsey Institute, whether reading erotic books
causes sexual crime or an appetite for sexual crime makes
people read erotic books. When the police search the house
of a man arrested for rape or indecent assault, they tend to
take possession of books they would ignore if the charge
against him were embezzlement, coining or falsification of
accounts. If they arrested me for rape, the likelihood of
which has now receded, they would find on my shelves a
number of books they would think highly significant. I have
seen in police possession, shamefacedly crammed together in
a Heinz tomato soup carton, a collection of books found in
the possession of a sex-murderer. Among them were many
that I remember seeing on the private shelves of a much-
respected Home Secretary. One of the most startling collec-
tions was found in the home of a public executioner who
committed suicide in 1947. The works of the Marquis de
Sade were found among the effects of Myra Hindley and
Brady, of the 'Moors Murders', in 1964. But it is idle to
pretend, as some lawyers will in defending obscenity cases,
that books do not influence the mind. Books are not directed
at the body. They teach, provoke, inspire to reflection and
sometimes to action.

So in recent years the Director of Public Prosecutions has
sought the aid of psychiatrists in deciding whether a book is
obscene, looked at in terms of mental health. A psychiatrist
will (I understand) consider the probable effect of such a
book on

(a) an adolescent, at the time when his sexual feeling may
not be clearly directed – and when he might be led to
imitate the kind of writing that has so stimulated him
and to pass it to others.

(b) a person with some latent perversion who may be
struggling to control his inclinations (and many
psychiatrists, aware of the importance of numbers, will

say that such people are far more numerous than the ordinary man would suppose).

(c) a potentially violent offender, whose sexuality may find an outlet in aggression.

By this test, very few novels incur the psychiatrists' condemnation: though some of them disapproved of *Last Exit to Brooklyn*, which they thought particularly likely to have an adverse effect on latent homosexuals, sometimes estimated as representing about 20 per cent of the male population. Other psychiatrists considered *Last Exit to Brooklyn* to be of no evil consequence, while yet others even thought it might be cathartic in its effect on readers already precariously balanced, relaxing tensions that could otherwise be socially dangerous. Other books sent by the D.P.P. to his psychiatric advisers concern themselves with the less dignified or less picturesque consequences of sexuality, and are usually non-scientific or pseudo-scientific. You will find these eccentricities described, with a naïvety that may be the effect of translation from the Swedish, in *The Erotic Minorities*, by Lars Ullerstam, M.D., published in 1967 by Calder & Boyars, London. But if you disapprove of all 'censorship' and you want to know whom to curse, some of your wrath should be reserved for these practitioners in psychological medicine, with whom the real responsibility often now resides. They are the new censors. They may not be ideal, but they didn't ask for the job and they seem to me preferable to the tinglings of Treasury Counsel.

There have been many versions of the 1954 'purge' and its origins. The police have been blamed, and the Public Morality Council, and a number of newspapers, and the then Home Secretary, Sir David Maxwell-Fyfe.[1] But the true account is probably the one given to the Select Committee of 1957 by Sir Theobald Matthew, the D.P.P. He was answering a question from Lord Lambton, who reminded him that he had declared it to be his policy '*not* normally to undertake prosecutions in respect of works written by reputable authors or published by reputable publishers'. How did this square with what had happened in 1954?

1. Later Lord Kilmuir.

One of them (said the D.P.P.) had been found by a court in the Isle of Man to be obscene, and was referred to me. I referred it to the Treasury Counsel, and he advised me that there was a *prima facie* case to be put before the Court. That was *The Philanderer*. It was acquitted. The other three cases[1] arose in this way. We were prosecuting in a case called *Reiter books* which, if I may say so, I don't think anybody could have argued were not pornographic. The defence in that case sought to put in a number of novels, including these three, which they said were as bad as, if not worse than, the ones which were being prosecuted, to show that public taste had changed. They were not allowed to put the books in, but an intimation was given, both in the court below and in the Court of Criminal Appeal, that those books might be looked at. That is not an intimation which I can ignore.

So all three were sent to Treasury Counsel and he thought they were obscene. There was a fourth called *Julia*, by Margot Bland, published by T. Werner Laurie, which seems to have got caught up in the rush.

Julia, a fairly straightforward love story in which the lovers perhaps ought to have known better, would never be convicted or even prosecuted today, and a conviction by jury would have been very unlikely then. But its publishers chose to cut their losses, pleaded guilty before the Magistrate at Clerkenwell and paid a fine of £30 and £10 costs. It was certainly much cheaper than a trial and an acquittal; for an acquitted publisher is seldom thought to merit an award of costs, which can run into four figures.

September in Quinze, by Vivian Connell, was really about September in Cannes, and concerned the Mediterranean amours of a Middle Eastern potentate whose recent dethronement had left him with idle hands and a lot of money. Both sides wanted the case dealt with by the Magistrate (Mr. Frank Milton at Marlborough Street) but he insisted on committing it for trial at the Old Bailey. He also, by the way, allowed the defence to put in some reviews and criticisms of

---

1. *The Image and the Search* (Heinemann); *September in Quinze* (Hutchinson); and *The Man in Control* (Barker).

the book, which were disallowed at the Old Bailey. There Mrs. Katherine Webb sat in the dock as a director of Hutchinson's (the Company also being a defendant). No one thought of bringing her out of the dock to sit with her solicitor, as had happened recently in the case of Mr. Fredric Warburg and *The Philanderer* (to which we will come in a moment); and if the temptation had occurred to the Judge (Sir Gerald Dodson, the Recorder of London), the following extract from his remarks in passing sentence may show why he found no difficulty in overcoming it:

> I should have thought any reader, however inexperienced, would have been repelled by a book of this sort, which is repugnant to every decent emotion which ever concerned man or woman.[1] It is a very comforting thought that juries from time to time take a very solid stand against this sort of thing, and realise how important it is for the youth of this country to be protected and that the fountain of our national blood should not be polluted at its source.

The Company and Mrs. Webb were fined £500 each.

'The Image and the Search'

The fountain of our national blood had been a genuine concern of the British delegates to the 1953 'Interpol' Conference mentioned earlier. They saw books as one of the causes of crime. The same idea was present to the mind of Mr. Justice Lynskey, who tried another of the famous 1954 cases, the publication by Heinemann of *The Image and the Search*, a novel by Walter Baxter. This was the story of a nymphomaniac, none too decorously portrayed, but extremely well written and commended in a private letter to the publisher by no less a critic than Mr. E. M. Forster as 'a serious and beautiful book'. Mr. Justice Lynskey presided at a second trial of this book, the first having ended in a failure of the jury to reach an agreement. (The first one was heard before Mr. Justice Devlin, and his impeccably fair summing-

---

1. This, I remember, caused some concern among women at the time, some of whom to my knowledge had rather enjoyed the book; and they wondered what the learned Recorder meant by 'however inexperienced' and whether, if they had been less experienced, they might have enjoyed it more.

D

up seemed to bear out the then popular theory – later invalidated by the *Chatterley* case – that if a judge tells an obscenity jury what to do they will do it, while if he sums up impartially they will disagree.) The defendants were Heinemann's, Mr. A. S. Frere (a director of the Company) and Mr. Baxter, the author. When Mr. Justice Lynskey came to address his jury, he began like this:

> This matter is a serious one, not only for the defendants but also for the general public. You need only look at my list at this Assize to see the kind of immorality of a criminal character that exists in this country. . . . You will realise that this is not an evil lightly to be brushed aside. It is an evil, if it exists, that has got to be cleaned up.

But it was 4.15 and the Judge decided not to try and finish that day. He broke off and said he would continue his summing-up in the morning. What he had said looked none too good in the evening papers, though no doubt the defence were discreetly rubbing their hands. No one had ever heard evidence that any book had led to any crime; and no one in particular had said that *The Image and the Search* was the cause of any of the crimes in Mr. Justice Lynskey's list at the 1954 Session of the Central Criminal Court. Left as it was, this would have been a 'misdirection' so fundamental that a verdict of guilty would be likely to result in a successful appeal. It was presumably Mr. Griffith Jones, for the Crown, who pointed this out to his Lordship overnight. In the morning, when he resumed his address to the jury, the judge returned to the subject of books and crime:

> When we adjourned last evening, I had endeavoured to point out to you the importance of this case from the point of view of the defendants, and also the general public; and I did refer, you may remember, to the type of cases I have had to try during this session. Well, I didn't want to suggest to you that this book had had anything whatever to do with those cases. It is perhaps a possible inference you might have drawn. Please don't. There is not a scintilla of evidence that any one of those people with whom I have had to deal has ever read the book, or seen it, or heard of it.

Or, he might have added, would have been induced if they had to go off and commit sexual outrages, incest and abortion – these being the crimes he had in mind. In the event, this jury disagreed, as the first one had.

True to a long-established tradition, a third jury was sworn in, told that it was going to hear no evidence whatever, and instructed to say 'Not Guilty'. This it dutifully and uneasily did. The publishers (and the author, for he was in the dock too) had been defended at the first trial by Mr. Rodger Winn, who had been so successful in *The Philanderer* case three months earlier. But before the second trial came on he had been appointed a Treasury Counsel and was not allowed to continue holding the brief (he is now Lord Justice Winn); and he was succeeded by Mr. Gerald Gardiner, Q.C., who is now Lord Chancellor. The case set no new standards, established no precedents: but 'expert evidence' of literary merit had been rather slyly adduced (to the vociferous disgust of the *Sunday Express*) in the form of the quoted letter from Mr. E. M. Forster. Between the two trials I had the following letter from one of the defendants, Mr. A. S. Frere, which I quote as illustrating the state of mind of a man who under our present obscenity laws does not know, and cannot know until the jury foreman or the Magistrate says Guilty, whether he has committed any offence at all:

99 Gt. Russell Street, W.C.1.
12.11.54.

Dear Mr. Rolph,

I believe you were in Court during the Old Bailey hearing. For a number of reasons which I think you will understand I have until now resisted my strong impulse to write to you. The prevalent view of publishers is that they are hard and successful; and therefore tough. And few people do not enjoy seeing a tough guy brought down a peg or two.

The curious thing about that Old Bailey dock is the feeling of overwhelming forces being ranged against you. You have been through the mill of long conferences with your own lawyers, and painfully learned to subordinate literary and moral considerations to the law as it stands. You learn how the machinery of the law can be rigged against you. You feel that, lacking the courage to be firm in the first place, you have landed a bewildered, ultra-sensitive and imaginative writer in the same mess with you. Your most intimate friends, probably from the best of motives, treat it as a huge joke. The only touch of human sympathy you encounter is from a cheerful little cockney jailer. The packed court gives you a curious feeling of inexorable censure. To a man – and woman – the jury look as if they will mercilessly run true to their own low standards. Awfully easy to be smitten by that most potent of human fears, being alone in the face of danger.

I do not know you by sight but I do know, now, that you were among several good friends in court that day. And I thank you most sincerely for your powerful and courageous public utterances about it all.[1] When they have the stage set to their own liking for a repeat per-formance, Baxter and I will feel so much strengthened and less alone, and I can't tell you how much it will help.

You may have heard that the Attorney-General has refused to allow Rodger Winn to go on with the case, which I believe is an unprecedented line for him to take. We are briefing Gerald Gardiner, whom I have not yet met but who, I am convinced, will fight well.

I set out to write you a letter of thanks. It seems to have turned into a personal whine, and for that I apologise. At any rate it is off my chest, and addressed to you whom I don't know, in the certainty that it will enlist your understanding.

Sincerely,
A. S. FRERE.

An aspect of the case which he may not then have foreseen, and which is further mentioned on p. 111 is that the defend-ants, as usual, were left to pay the whole of their considerable costs for the three trials; a heavy price to pay for the vindi-cation of a book which (unlike *Chatterley*) has passed almost into limbo.

'The Man in Control'

The prosecution of Arthur Barker Ltd. for publishing *The Man in Control* was an event that made lawyers as well as

---

1. I think this must have been because I had written articles saying that the book censorship system was daft. – C.H.R.

publishers scratch their heads even in 1954. The theme of the book was roughly that of *The Well of Loneliness*.[1] The author, Charles McGraw, had died before the question of prosecution arose, and the only defendant to be sat in the dock (as a director of the Company) was Mr. Herbert van Thal, an eminently likeable and clubbable man known to every publisher as a lover of English literature. Again, no one suggested he should come out of the dock and sit with his solicitor. Even a felon does this in the Californian courts, which are not built on zoological principles. He stayed in the cage with his jailer, and none of us ran the risk of contamination. He was tried by Judge Aarvold, who allowed the jury to see (or if not the jury, then everyone else in court) that he himself thought the prosecution rather silly. The jury retired for 12 minutes and came back to say 'Not Guilty'. Costs? No costs were allowed. The publishers were lucky to be prosecuted.

'The Philanderer'

I have left *The Philanderer* until last, although in point of time it was the second of the five trials of 1954, because it was by far the most influential, and it was the summing-up by Mr. Justice Stable that really precipitated the coming change in the law. The American author, Stanley Kauffman, was not in Court. The defendants were Secker & Warburg Ltd., publishers, Mr. Fredric Warburg, one of their directors, and the printers of the book, Camelot Press Ltd. (who would not, under modern practice, be prosecuted). The sole occupant of the dock, however, was Mr. Warburg. Mr. Justice Stable had no intention of keeping him there. He invited him down into the well of the court, where he could sit with his solicitors; and then told the jury he had no intention of keeping them in *their* box either – they could take the book home and read it. 'Read it *as a book*', he told them. 'Don't pick out the highlights. Read it through as a whole. And then we'll all come back here on Friday and proceed with the case.' But both Counsel made speeches before they went. Mr.

1. See p. 76.

Mervyn Griffith-Jones said the book was published 15 months earlier, that 6,000 copies had been sold, and that he was going to ask the jury to say when they had read it that it would have a 'tendency to deprave and corrupt those whose minds were open to such immoral influences and into whose hands it might fall'.

All that kind of thing, said Mr. Rodger Winn for the defence, was 150 years old. One had to move with the times. And the Judge seemed to strike a challenging opening chord when he said that the problem was going to be whether the impact of certain passages on a Victorian mind would be the same as on a modern mind.

> I remember [said Mr. Justice Stable] a most serious discussion between my mother and father, whether my mother could possibly go and see Mr. Shaw's play *Pygmalion*. When the lady in the play said 'Not bloody likely' it was the biggest social shock I can remember. If I had used that word when I was 21, I would have been ordered out of any respectable house in England.[1]

There is reason to believe that the education of that jury and many future ones took place during that short speech. Here was a Judge of the Queen's Bench Division saying bloody and implying that, though wrong when he was 21, it was all right now. What else might be all right? They went away to read the book.

During the trial no expert witness was called on either side. Mr. Justice Stable might well have allowed it on the strength of *de Montalk's* case,[2] but the attempt was not made. Instead there were some distinguished literary figures to be seen among the 'public' in Court No. 2 at the Old Bailey, and the jury were noticeably aware of them because some of them were television personalities. What were they there for, a juryman might well ask himself? Not, you could be sure, to say that the book was irredeemably obscene.

It had been well reviewed, and the notices had seemed to give it the blessing due to a book that 'condemned what it

1. Mr. Justice Stable was 21 in 1909. I was eight. I remember thinking that 'bloody' was said only by drunken flower-sellers on Saturday nights. – C.H.R.
2. See p. 83.

portrayed'.[1] Mr. Walter Allen in the *New Statesman* of 25th April 1953 had said that he found in it

> as devastating a criticism as any I've read of the conse-
> quences of the tradition of American adolescent competi-
> tion in sexual experience that we have already had
> described for us by Dr. Margaret Mead and Mr. Gorer.

The jury may not have seen this but, since that was the general tone of critical comment on the book, the Judge would be likely to be aware of it. The book had already been condemned (with *Julia*[2]) in the Isle of Man, where the police received a complaint that you could get it from Boots' Library. The High Bailiff, considering himself to be bound by a law which he regarded as outmoded, had deprecatingly imposed fines of £1 on *The Philanderer* and £1 on *Julia*. *Julia's* fate in England we have already witnessed; and now there was *The Philanderer* with an I.O.M. criminal record too.

As expected, Mr. Justice Stable's summing-up to the jury was strongly sympathetic, not to the book itself (which he clearly didn't think much of) but to the defendants in being accused as criminals for publishing it. The summing-up was full of such rhetorical questions as these – each being followed by 'it's a matter for you, members of the jury':

1. Corrupt or deprave whom?
2. A fourteen-year-old schoolgirl?
3. A child in the nursery?
4. Is it books that put ideas into young people's heads?
5. Or is it nature?
6. Do the unmarried women in New York believe that babies are
   - (a) brought by storks?
   - (b) found in cabbage plots?
   - (c) found under gooseberry bushes?
7. Is the act of sexual passion 'sheer filth'?
8. If we drive the criminal law too far, in our desire to stamp out the 'bawdy muck', isn't there a risk that there will be a revolt, *a demand for a change in the law,* '*so that the pendulum may swing too far the other way and allow to creep in things that at the moment we can keep out*'?

1. And was therefore not pornographic (see p. 44).
2. See p. 96.

The verdict was 'Not Guilty'. The defendants were discharged (again without any costs being awarded) and the stage was set for a law reform movement.

It is true that, since the Stable summing-up was not a Court of Appeal judgment, it was binding on no one. It had 'persuasive authority' only. But such a decisive lead has sometimes been sufficient, even without Court of Appeal authority, to change the course of the law; an instance being *R. v. Bourne*, which in 1939 established that a doctor could perform legally an abortion to save the health (and not only to save the life) of the mother. The broad implications of the Stable summing-up were sturdily ignored by Sir Gerald Dodson in *September in Quinze*, by many magistrates making destruction orders in the next few years, and of course by the customs and postal authorities in making their seizures of books in transit; but the wind had changed.

The Literary World

The alarm in the literary and publishing world was widespread, genuine and well-founded. The judicial resistance to Mr. Justice Stable's views, though far from unanimous, showed that 1954 *could* happen all over again. The Society of Authors combined with members of the Publishers Association, representatives of the printing world, and literary agents to form a law-reform committee to 'examine the existing law of obscene libel and to recommend reforms'. Its chairman was Sir Alan Herbert and its vice-chairman Sir Gerald Barry. Its members were Walter Allen, H. E. Bates, David Carver, Professor Guy Chapman, W. B. Clowes, W. A. R. Collins, Joseph Compton, Rupert Hart-Davis, Roy Jenkins, M.P., A. D. Peters, V. S. Pritchett, John Pudney, Sir Herbert Read, Denys Kilham Roberts, Norman St. John Stevas, and W. E. (now Sir William Emrys) Williams. Its honorary secretary was C. H. Rolph.

It is relevant here to repeat the words of the Attorney-General (Sir Hartley Shawcross) when he was answering questions in the House of Commons in May 1949 concerning *The Naked and the Dead*:

While there is much in this most tedious and lengthy book which is foul, lewd and revolting, looking at it as a whole I do not think its intent is to corrupt or deprave – *or that it is likely to lead to any other result than disgust.*

'Intent', therefore, which had once been an essential ingredient in, but had lately disappeared from, the criminal offence of 'obscene libel', seemed to be coming back; and the idea of disgust as something more easily comprehensible than depravity or corruption had been given a first legal airing. It was in this atmosphere that the 1954 prosecutions, and their general appearance of failure, had to be considered. The 'Herbert Committee' decided to try and get rid of the '*tendency* to deprave and corrupt' principle and to substitute the need to consider whether the 'general character and dominant effect' of a book, etc., was corrupting. Towards this end, the Committee's draft Bill would have *allowed* evidence of actually corrupting effect (though no one knew quite what this would be) and *required* evidence either that this was the publisher's (or author's) intention or that he was indifferent and careless about what effect the book might have.

The first Draft Bill

The relevant clauses of the first Bill said that no one was to be convicted unless

(a) the accused *intended* to corrupt the persons to or among whom the obscene matter was intended or was likely to be distributed, etc. (which no one really thought likely to be susceptible of proof); or

(b) in so distributing, etc., he was reckless as to whether the obscene matter would or would not have a corrupting effect upon such persons.

The Court would be required to consider the 'general character and dominant effect' of the book, and to listen to expert evidence about its literary or artistic merit, or its 'medical, legal, political, religious or scientific character or importance'. The Bill abolished the common law offence of obscene libel; and it said that the word 'obscene' was to include 'any matter which, whether or not related to any sexual context, unduly exploits horror, cruelty, or violence, whether pictorially or otherwise'. There was to be no prosecution without the consent of the Attorney-General, and every case would be disposed of by Magistrates unless the defendant wanted trial by jury, which was made available to him by setting a term of imprisonment (there was also a fine of £100) at a maximum of four months. (Any criminal charge carrying 'more than three months' imprisonment' automatically confers an option of jury trial.) The Parliamentary sponsors of the Bill were Mr. Roy Jenkins, Mr. (later Sir) John Foster, Q.C., Mr. Michael Foot, Mr. Angus Maude, Mrs. Eirene White, Mr. Nigel Nicolson, Mr. Kenneth Robinson, and Mr. Jocelyn Simon, Q.C. (now Sir Jocelyn Simon, President of the Divorce Division of the High Court). Mr. Jenkins introduced the Bill under the 'ten-minute rule' in March 1955. He got no further, but the Home Office, showing a cautious desire to co-operate, offered suggestions for its improvement. Mr. Hugh Fraser presented the next version (only slightly modified) in November of the same year, and it was 'talked out'.

'Horror Comics'

At about this time the Home Office, suddenly abandoning its attitude of helpful neutrality, bowed to a storm of protest about imported American 'horror comics' and brought in a Bill of its own to ban them. This became the Children and Young Persons (Harmful Publications) Act 1955, and penalised:

> any book, magazine or other like work which is of a kind likely to fall into the hands of children or young persons and consists wholly or mainly of stories told in pictures (with or without the addition of written matter), being stories portraying
>
> (a) the commission of crimes, or
> (b) acts of violence or cruelty, or
> (c) incidents of a repulsive or horrible nature,

in such a way that the work as a whole would tend to corrupt a child or young person into whose hands it might fall.

This covered some of the same ground as the Herbert Committee's Bill; and though that was the ground in which its promoters were really the least interested, this new and unheralded move had the disturbing appearance of a Home Office bid to steal its thunder and make it seem less urgently necessary. But in March 1957, Lord Lambton, drawing a good place in the Ballot for private members' time, brought it in again, secured a second reading for it a fortnight later, and then (a most unexpected triumph and an augury of promise) saw it referred to a Select Committee which began work on it, under the chairmanship of Sir Patrick Spens, in May of the same year.

The Select Committee's Report

The Bill then lapsed with that Session of Parliament; but the Select Committee, which was about half-way through the business of hearing witnesses, went on in the new Session to complete its examination, not indeed of the now defunct Bill but of the issues which it had raised. Its report is an encouragingly liberal document, and with the supporting *Minutes of Evidence* it constitutes the fullest available exposition of the 'censorship' laws as they existed at that time – and, to a large extent, as they still exist today.

The Herbert Committee promptly gave expression to this Report in a freshly-drafted Bill, now in the capable hands again of Mr. Roy Jenkins. And it was this version on which, at last and in real earnest, battle was joined behind the scenes with the Home Office legal advisers and the Law Officers of the Crown, the former being in the main helpful, the latter relentlessly obstructive.

The final product, The Obscene Publications Act of 1959, included a number of provisions (they are discussed on p. 18) which the Society of Authors and the Bill's other supporters had accepted with great reluctance, and only because continued opposition to them would have meant the loss of the Bill altogether.

The Defence of 'Public Good'

However, Parliament had accepted for the first time the notion that although a book might be obscene, that is to say it might tend to deprave and corrupt, its publication could nevertheless be for the public good:

> A person shall not be convicted of (publishing an obscene article) and an order for forfeiture shall not be made, if it is proved that publication of the article in question is justified as being for the public good on the ground that it is in the interests of science, literature, art or learning, or of other objects of general concern.

Within a year the Act was being tested at the Central Criminal Court. Penguin Books Limited were prosecuted for publishing a 3s. 6d. paperback of *Lady Chatterley's Lover*. They had told the police they were going to publish it, in fulfilment of their plan to publish the whole of D. H. Lawrence's works.

Thirty-five expert witnesses – literary critics, theologians, moralists, university dons, priests, publishers, authors – gave evidence that its publication was 'for the public good'.

Mr. Justice Byrne, though visibly unimpressed by most of them, resolved a number of legal arguments in a way that surprisingly advanced the boundaries of literary freedom; and so far those rulings have not come before the Court of Appeal for consideration in any subsequent case. He agreed, for example, that although an author's intention was irrelevant to the question of *obscenity* (see p. 93), it could be important – and was admissible – in relation to the literary, artistic or other merits by which that obscenity might be redeemed or excused. 'One has to have regard,' his Lordship said, 'to what the author was trying to do, what his message may have been, and what his general scope was.' That amounts to a present to any lawyer defending an obscenity case in the future, but so far as one can judge from the law reports it seems to have been overlooked. The same can be said of another ruling that 'the literary merits of this book' (i.e. *Lady Chatterley's Lover*) 'can be dealt with by comparing it with the literary merit or otherwise of other books.' This was getting very close to what Mr. Reiter's lawyers (see

p. 96) had wanted when they 'sought to put in a number of novels which they said were as bad as, if not worse than, the ones being prosecuted, to show that public taste had changed'. Not only were they not allowed to do it, but the books they were proposing to do it with were all sent to the Director of Public Prosecutions and prosecuted in their turn. Nothing in the 1959 Act specifically allows such comparisons; but a persuasive precedent has nevertheless been established by a criminal law Judge of great experience who was notoriously careful in his use of words.

The jury believed the 35 expert witnesses and said 'Not Guilty'; but the acquittal cost Penguin Books the sum of £13,000 and the Judge refused, although it was acknowledged to be a 'test case', to make an order (as he could have done) that they be reimbursed from public funds.[1]

Defects in the 1959 Act

Certain snags now began to appear in the path of the new Act and those who would enforce it. First, display in a shop window was not 'an offer for sale'; it was merely an 'invitation to treat' (*Mella* v. *Monahan,* 1961); a snag that had necessitated in 1961 an amendment to a similar provision in the 'Flick-Knives' Act (the Restriction of Offensive Weapons Act, 1959).

Secondly, the clock was put right back in relation to publisher's 'intent' by the *Ladies' Directory* case in 1961 (*R.* v. *Shaw*) – 'the test of obscenity depends on the publication itself and the intention of the publisher is irrelevant.' Thirdly, supplying the book to a police officer was not an offence; nothing could tend to deprave and corrupt a policeman, or at any rate a policeman who was a member of the 'vice squad' (*R.* v. *Clayton and Halsey,* 1962). So Penguin Books could never have been rightly convicted, after all, even if the jury rejected all the expert witnesses: the twelve copies of *Lady Chatterley* which they were prosecuted for publishing had all been handed (by the most gentlemanly arrangement conceivable) to a police officer from the vice

1. The *Chatterley* case is conveniently reported, with annotations, in *The Trial of Lady Chatterley,* Penguin Books, London, 1961.

squad. Fourthly, in a case involving *Cain's Book*, by Alexander Trocchi, 'obscenity' was held to include drug-addiction, so that 'tendency to corrupt' could include making people want to take drugs (*R. v. John Calder Publications Ltd.*, 1965).

Some of these developments and difficulties, with others that brought into existence, in 1963, the 'London Committee against Obscenity',[1] were ironed out by a further Obscene Publications Act of 1964, the main provision in which was the creation of a new offence – '*having* an obscene article for publication for gain'. This, in making it possible for the police to prosecute a publisher who merely *possessed* (for publication for gain) a lot of undeniably obscene magazines, unfortunately made it possible also to prosecute the best of publishers for having stocks (for publication for gain) of any book disliked by the police, by any private citizen, or by the magistrates.

'*Last Exit to Brooklyn*'

In 1967, Sir Cyril Black, M.P. (who is an official of the Social Morality Council) took out a summons against a London bookseller for having copies of *Last Exit to Brooklyn*. It called upon him, within the terms of Section 3 of the Obscene Publications Act, 1959, to 'show cause why the said books should not be forfeited' (or, in other words, burned). This procedure had been expressly preserved in the 1959 Act because the then Attorney-General had mercifully said there were cases in which he wanted merely to suppress a book rather than to punish the publisher.

A number of literary critics and other experts said in evidence that the publication of *Last Exit to Brooklyn* was for the public good, but a number of others said that it wasn't; and this was the first time, since such a thing became possible, that any of the experts had been on the side of the authorities. The Magistrate agreed with those on the complainant's (i.e. Sir Cyril Black's) side, and three copies of *Last Exit to Brooklyn* were burnt. Sir Cyril Black had taken action because the Attorney-General, Sir Elwyn Jones, speaking in the House of Commons, had declined to do so.

1. See p. 15.

The Magistrate's decision merely meant that copies of the book found *in that Magistrate's area* could now be seized and burned – elsewhere they could have an even merrier (if that is the word) sale. But Calder & Boyars, the publishers, forced the issue by announcing that they, notwithstanding the local effect of the Bow Street condemnation, were going ahead with the production and distribution of the book; and the Attorney-General, rising at last to the bait, took out a summons against them under Section 2 of the 1959 Act (as amended in 1964) for 'possessing an obscene article for gain'.

Thus at last, in November 1967, *Last Exit to Brooklyn* was before an Old Bailey jury. After a nine-day trial they returned a verdict of Guilty. Mr. John Calder afterwards said (*The Times*, 2nd December 1967) that 'the prosecution treated the trial as a gentlemenly test case, confined itself to the main issues and did not drag in others involving prejudice, while the Judge, in his summing-up, reviewed the evidence very impartially. But nothing', Mr. Calder went on, 'can be precisely known of the capabilities of juries dealing with such cases ... In the new climate in which publishers and writers now find themselves, where highly complex literary concepts will be argued out in criminal courts, it is essential that the framers of the Obscene Publications Act should bring in a new provision that enables juries to be selected from those who have at least A-levels in their education and who can show to the satisfaction of the court that they are capable of reading and understanding the book they have to judge.' Mr. Calder's just complaint about semi-literate jurors is an indictment of the jury system as a whole, which nothing short of a revolution is likely to change. Many a jury trying a complicated commercial fraud has included members to whom the whole story was totally unintelligible. A complaint rather more susceptible of remedy was that the cost of the Calder & Boyars defence and the appeal hearing, undertaken very largely in the public interest, was not much short of £20,000, beside which the fine of £100 was totally insignificant. If Calder & Boyars had lost their appeal, this is what they would have had to find. By a lucky accident they won, and we will consider the accident in a moment. It was no accident, though it was even luckier, that the Judges gave them their appeal costs.

The costs problem had already been discovered, by Sir Cyril Black, to present snags for the private prosecutor. During the debates on the final Bill in the House of Commons, its promoters' disappointment at not getting the Director of Public Prosecutions made statutorily responsible was assuaged by a Government concession that unsuccessful private prosecutors (if they were thought, in effect, to be meddling busy-bodies) *could* be ordered to pay their own costs. This duly went into the Act as Section 3 (6). What was omitted from the Act, and is dealt with in no other, was what happens when the private complaint *succeeds*. Sir Cyril Black succeeded; and the Magistrate, to his own surprise no less than to Sir Cyril Black's, was unable to award him any costs. They amounted to about £1,000.

The Court of Appeal did not decide that *Last Exit to Brooklyn* was not obscene. Nor did it decide that, even if obscene, its publication was for the public good. These are matters that, under English law and procedure, no Court of Appeal will ever decide: they are both 'matters for the jury alone'. It decided, in effect, that the case had not been properly tried and that, accordingly, the conviction could not stand. This was because Judge Rogers at the Old Bailey 'had not put a word of the specific defence to the jury when summing up on the issue of obscenity'; and in particular had not explained to the jury that they must consider three vital matters:

1. Whether the tendency of the book might be to deprave and corrupt 'a significant proportion of those persons likely to read it'. (And much will be heard, in future trials, of those unprecedented words about 'a significant proportion' of readers. A handful of 'corrupted' witnesses, even if they can be found, will never be enough. The principle is the one laid down in *Pearce's Case* by Mr. Justice Tindal Atkinson (it was a quarrel between a landowner and the Railways and Canals Commission); namely that 'the word public must be treated as comprising a considerable body of persons'.)

2. What the tendency of the book was alleged to be. The defence had said it was 'compassionate and con-

demnatory': it was 'admittedly and intentionally
disgusting, shocking and outrageous', so that the reader,
being now made aware of the truth, might be moved to
'do what he could to eradicate these evils and the
conditions in modern society which so callously allowed
them to exist'. The defence had also said (in flat
contradiction of the psychiatric evidence outlined on
page 94) that 'instead of tending to encourage anyone
to homosexuality, drug taking, or senseless, brutal
violence it would have precisely the opposite effect'.

3. How it is possible for a book with 'corrupting and
depraving tendencies' to be justified as being 'for
the public good'. Lord Justice Salmon said that a
jury, with no explanation as to the true meaning of
the Statute in this regard, 'may well be left in a state
of perplexity'. Judge Rogers at the Old Bailey had in
effect, his Lordship said, 'thrown them in at the deep
end' of this particular problem and 'left them to sink
or swim in its dark waters'.

So there has never been any final decision about the
obscenity of *Last Exit to Brooklyn*, or its redemption by social
or literary value. There never will be, because a Court of
Appeal acquittal has the same total finality as a jury's
acquittal. It could make no difference now if Mr. John
Calder were to say at some time in the future: 'Now it can be
told. I've been fooling everyone. This book is squalidly
obscene and was meant to be, its literary value is nil, its story
baseless, its social commentary humbug. It will undoubtedly
do a lot of harm, but I can't help that – I was concerned
merely to expose the fatuity of the law.' If Mr. Calder now
told us that, the law could but gnash its teeth at him. *Last
Exit* can now go on making its readers impotently sick or
belligerently angry for as long as ever they find it worth the
money.

But its imitators, successors and out-doers face a clarified
legal situation. For the first time since the passing of the 1959
Act, every trial Judge will now find the essence of his
summing-up written for him. (And from it, every Magistrate
will know how he is to direct his mind.) Here it is in the words
of Lord Justice Salmon:

E

You must consider on the one hand, members of the jury, the number of readers you believe would tend to be corrupted by this book; then the strength of its tendency to corrupt and deprave; and then the nature of that corruption and depravity. On the other hand you must assess the strength of the literary, sociological or ethical merit which you consider the book to possess. You must then weigh up all these factors and decide whether on balance the publication is proved to be justified as being for the public good. A book may be worthless; a book may have slight but real merit; it may be a work of genius. Between these extremes the gradations are almost infinite. A book may tend to deprave and corrupt a significant but comparatively small number of its readers or a large number or, indeed, the majority of its readers. The tendency to corrupt may be strong or slight. The corruption may also take various forms. It may be to induce erotic desires of a heterosexual kind, or to promote homosexuality or other sexual perversions, or drug-taking or brutal violence. All these are matters for you to consider and weigh up. It is for you to decide, in the light of the importance you attach to these factors, whether or not the publication is for the public good. You must set the standards of what is acceptable, of what is for the public good in the age in which we live.

And from that archetypal summing-up the Director of Public Prosecutions, the police, lawyers asked to advise, publishers hesitating over manuscripts, booksellers weighing pros and cons – all will be able to draw lessons and inferences never before available. Prosecutions will be easier but less likely.

The Right to Trial by Jury

One respect in which the sponsors of the 1959 Act have always considered it to have failed is that it continues to withhold, in these 'destruction order' cases, the right of trial by jury. There seemed to be no better reason for this particular injustice than the fact that that was the way it had always been. Two pressure groups had been urging Mr. Roy Jenkins, when he became Home Secretary, to introduce amending legislation. One group wanted to take away from private persons this right to bring 'destruction order' actions on their own whenever they felt like it. The other wanted such actions to be triable by jury if the defendants felt like that. Mr. Jenkins, to a chorus of disapproval from strictly constitutional lawyers, placated the former faction (but not the latter), by means of the last-minute insertion in the Criminal Justice Act, 1967, referred to on page 22.

Legislative Odds and Ends

Literary matters apart, there are untidy remnants of Statute law occasionally used to prosecute 'obscenity' at art exhibitions. There have lately been police raids on art exhibitions. In February 1967, an Edinburgh Magistrate decided that a number of Aubrey Beardsley prints, seized in a local shop, were indecent. He was not being asked to say that they were obscene, within the meaning of the Obscene Publications Act 1959, probably because that would have let in expert evidence about artistic merit redounding to the public good. Instead the charge was laid under a 1961 Edinburgh Corporation By-law prohibiting the display of 'indecent or obscene' books or pictures for sale.

When the Society of Authors' first draft Bill was presented by Mr. Roy Jenkins in 1955, it contained a schedule of repeals that would have got rid of local enactments conflicting with it or covering the same ground. For a variety of reasons, chiefly the constitutional tradition against wide-ranging 'consolidation' Statutes being initiated by private members, these repeals were whittled down, and finally even Section 4 of the Vagrancy Act 1824 was allowed to survive. This penalises 'every person wilfully exposing to view in any public place or in the window or other part of any shop or other building situate in any public place any obscene print, picture or other indecent exhibition'. In 1966 the Magistrate at Great Marlborough Street, in London, held that a display of collages by the American artist, Jim Dine, put on in a West End picture gallery, was punishably indecent under the Vagrancy Act – a policeman had been just able to see them through a window from the street. The 1824 Vagrancy Act is coming back into police favour as a means of controlling this art business, because the word 'indecent' has attracted less hair-splitting ingenuity than the word 'obscene'. It is true that in December 1966, the Leeds Magistrate decided that some paintings by Stass Paraskos, a Greek Cypriot artist, were obscene within the meaning of the 1959 Act (i.e. that they 'tended to deprave and corrupt'), and that their obscenity was not artistic enough to be for the public good.

But in February 1965 the Lord Chief Justice, in the Court of Criminal Appeal, had held (in a case under the Post Office Act) that a cine-film sent through the mail was indecent although it was not obscene. The two words, said the Lord Chief Justice, convey one idea, 'namely, offending against the recognised standards of propriety, with indecency at the lower end of the scale and obscenity at the upper end'.

What Remains to be Done

There is thus a clearing-up job to be done, even if it achieves no more than to rationalise the law as it stands at present. All the local and minor and loose-end statutory provisions should be killed off and then (if they ever had any value) re-enacted in a consolidation measure. And the surviving bits of the Common Law should be killed off *without* being re-enacted anywhere. This is true particularly of the law of conspiracy in any form, whether to 'corrupt public morals' (as in the *Ladies' Directory* case) or to contravene the Obscene Publications Act, in which form it is probably an effective means of silencing any tiresome expert evidence about literary and other 'public good' defences.

VI

SOME PROPOSALS
FOR REFORM

And that, roughly speaking, is where we came in. The extent of the 'clearing up job' has been indicated, in previous pages, by a mere selection from a large number of court cases, some of which became causes célèbres and some not. The post-1959 peaks, in terms of notoriety though not necessarily of legal significance, were *Lady Chatterley's Lover*, *Fanny Hill* and *Last Exit to Brooklyn*. But the proceedings[1] in 1965 against *Cain's Book*, by Alexander Trocchi, created some uncertainty about the scope of the word 'obscene', and it is an uncertainty that ought to be removed. This book was among a number seized by the police in a Sheffield bookshop, and they moved the Magistrates to summon the shopkeeper to show cause why it should not be destroyed. It was about the life of a New York drug addict; it was not obscene in the usual sense of the word, but could be said to be corrupting if it might induce its readers to become junkies. A number of literary people thought it sufficiently meritorious to justify their journey to Sheffield as 'expert witnesses' to the effect that its publication could redound to the public good. The magistrates decided (a) that the word obscene did not have to be confined in its meaning to any sexual context, and (b) that they were entitled, even if they accepted the experts' views, to say that the 'public good' defence had not been made out to their satisfaction – the obscenity (i.e., incitement to drug-taking) outweighed the literary excellence and the quality of the social commentary. And this the Queen's Bench Judges upheld on appeal. The odd thing was that Parliament itself,

1. *John Calder (Publications) Ltd* v. *Powell*, 1965.

in the very year in which this case was decided, were taking the view that 'obscene' did not include non-sexual forms of corruption, depravity or deviation and, for that reason, passed the Children and Young Persons (Harmful Publications) Act 1955, to deal with 'horror comics'. There is a conflict here between Parliament and the courts that ought to be resolved.

Before going on, however, to the general reforms that have similarly been shown to be necessary, one should at least glance at the one that will remain impracticable just so long as 'sex' retains its prurient interest, which promises to be a long time. This is that the newspapers should call the dogs off. From among the 'non-prosecutions', the big fish that have got away, let us select the case of *Lolita*, by Vladimir Nabokov, published in England by Weidenfeld and Nicolson in 1959, while (again) the law was actually in the process of changing. *Lolita's* build-up started when the *Sunday Times*, at Christmas 1955, asked a number of prominent people what they thought were the best books of the year just ending. Among Mr. Graham Greene's choices was *Lolita*, then available only from the Olympia Press in France. Four American publishers had turned it down, and the French edition was not doing very well.

But who should be thus induced to procure a copy but Mr. John Gordon of the *Sunday Express*! He got it from France. 'It is the filthiest book I have ever read,' he announced in his column on the 29th January 1956, when he had finished it. 'It is sheer unrestrained pornography,' he went on. 'Anyone who published or sold it here would certainly go to prison.' The Home Office, having read its *Sunday Express*, persuaded the French to ban the book under the Geneva Convention. *Lolita* was made. Holland published it, and Sweden, Denmark, Western Germany, Spain (usually fairly timid), Italy, Portugal and Japan. The film rights were sold for a fortune. There had been an Israeli edition in 1955. The Preface to its second reprint, in 1957, contained this interesting statement:

When the manuscript was submitted to us in the Spring of 1955 we immediately decided to publish it. . . . Publication in September 1955 was followed by complete silence. For many months, sales were ridiculously low – until *Lolita* received publicity from an unexpected quarter. This meant John Gordon's condemnation in the *Sunday Express*. Never, said the Israeli publishers, had the machinations of censorship been so perfectly demonstrated:

Lolita certainly owes its present fame more to its adventurous and unconventional beginning than to its intrinsic qualities. The book would never have met with such success had not the John Gordons of this world scared American publishers into rejecting it in the first place.

In 1959 Weidenfeld & Nicholson contrived to extract from the then Attorney-General a *sub rosa* undertaking that the book would not be prosecuted if published in this country. This, it is almost certain, was due neither to any change in the policy by which the Law Officers consistently decline to act as publishers' advisers, nor to an official view that *Lolita* was all right. It was much more probably based on the view that such a prosecution at that time would have stirred up powerful sympathies against the Government's clauses in the Obscene Publications Bill, which they thought were going rather well. The Society of Authors and the Herbert Committee thought it might do similar damage to *their* favourite clauses. So there was a gentlemanly postponement for a month or two. *Lolita's* appearance was, in fact, impeccably and artfully timed. But its success was a Fleet Street 'promotion'.[1]

I propose now to examine, in conclusion, some alternative suggestions (including one or two of my own) for reforming the law and procedure. Some of these seem to me good and and practical, some ill-conceived and impractical. I start with the latter.

Some Impractical Proposals

THAT ALL CENSORSHIP BE ABOLISHED

The proponents of this idea usually say 'Let the public decide'. What public? They are thinking not even of the

1. Similarly, in Elinor Glyn's 'breach of copyright' action in 1916 (see p. 69), Mr. Justice Younger remarked that her book *Three Weeks* had been 'fortunate enough to be condemned almost unanimously by the critics and to be banned by all the libraries.'

whole reading public but of that section wanting the kind of books the fuss is all about. The public as a whole probably wants censorship, wants to feel that its sexy books are contraband and that someone (i.e., somebody else) could be punished if the police knew. The champions of liberty are blinded by their own controversies and deafened by their own vociferousness to the fact that they are a tiny self-regarding community. And if the public doesn't want censorship now, it would want it suddenly and angrily if it found that anyone could publish, display and distribute whatever he liked. There are countries – Denmark is the latest – where this drastic step has been taken, and the experiment is being watched with interest. In England there is a 'thought-barrier' to be broken through before this becomes an even remote possibility, and it is at least as old as the great Rebellion and the descent of the Puritan darkness, following the discovery that sex was being actually enjoyed and had better be recognised for what it was, a manifestation of evil. There are also people responsible for the care, training and education of the young who wage a constant battle against pornography – heads of schools in particular. And there are modern sexologists who ask why these anxious people should waste their nervous energy in such a war: the prohibition (they say) does more harm than good. The latter view may eventually prevail, though the thought barrier it will have to get through looks almost impenetrable; and if I were a prosperous pornographer, I would be looking forward to it with apprehension and making arrangements for a rapid switch to another form of business.

OBSCENITY CASES SHOULD BE TRIED ONLY BY ASCERTAINABLY LITERATE JURORS

This is the heartfelt view of Mr. John Calder, publisher in England of *Last Exit to Brooklyn*.[1] It has a respectable ancestry, to go no further back than the words of Sir James Fitzjames Stephen, written in 1883:

> Whatever the fashion of the times may say to the contrary, I think that the great bulk of the working classes are

1. See p. 111.

altogether unfit to discharge judicial duties; nor do I believe that, rare exceptions excepted, a man who has to work hard all day long at a mechanical trade will ever have either the memory or the mental power, or the habits of thought necessary to retain, analyse and arrange in his mind the evidence of, say, twenty witnesses to a number of minute facts given, perhaps, on two different days. Jurors almost never take notes, and most of them would only confuse themselves by any attempt to do; and I strongly suspect that a large proportion of them would, if examined openly at the end of a trial as to the different matters which they had heard in the course of it, be found to be in a state of hopeless confusion and bewilderment. I should be far from saying this of good *special* juries; but I think that the habit of flattering and encouraging the poor, and asserting that they are just as sensible and capable of performing judicial and political functions as those who from their infancy have had the advantages of leisure, education and wealth, has led to views as to the persons qualified to be jurors which may be very mischievous. I think that in all criminal cases of any considerable difficulty or importance there ought to be at least a power to summon special juries.[1]

Not that there were many 'rude mechanicals' on juries in Stephen's time: the qualifications were such that jurors came mostly from the landed gentry. The enfranchisement of the millions has since brought some even ruder mechanicals into jury boxes. If liability for jury service is to be extended to all those entitled to vote at elections; if that right to vote is to be the sole qualification for jury service; and if the right to vote is to be accorded to all who have reached the age of eighteen years, then we shall have juries of teenagers who have finished with formal education but are without even a rude mechanical's experience of the world they are still growing up in. And all these, as I write, are serious government proposals.

'Special juries' were abolished even in civil cases after the Laski libel action in 1946; and their revival, for either civil or criminal trials, is even less likely than the abolition of the

1. *History of the Criminal Law of England*, Vol. 1, pp 571/2. London, 1883.

jury system altogether. But since the introduction of 'expert evidence' in obscenity trials it has certainly become apparent that an ordinary jury is not the best tribunal to determine the future of English literature.

A defendant has an early opportunity to assess the literary standards of the jurors who are going to try him. It occurs when they severally take the oath at the very beginning; and it is rare, even today, for a jury to be without two or three members who seem barely able to read and must be conducted through the little oath-taking ceremony by the court usher. I do not know why we go on pretending to each other that this is a good system of administering justice; or why today our leading jurists lack the forthrightness of Mr. Justice Stephen. But there *is* a means by which something approximating to a special jury can, by unorthodox means, be contrived. The court officials know the professions and occupations of all the jurors summoned to the court. If they know that a certain trial is to begin on a certain date, they can defer until that date the empanelling of a sufficient number of waiting jurors who are qualified to understand it. And they do.

But this is as near as we shall get to 'special juries'; and perhaps it is even nearer than we ought to get.

THAT NO BOOK SHOULD BE PROSECUTED WITHOUT THE APPROVAL OF A HOME OFFICE COMMITTEE OF 'LITERATE PERSONS SPECIALLY SELECTED FOR THE PURPOSE'

This is the proposal of Lord Goodman, chairman of the Arts Council of Great Britain[1]; and as well as a growing number of adherents it has attracted a growing number of vociferous critics. Publishers are chary of adjudicating panels. New Zealand now has an Indecent Publications Committee, set up by Statute and charged with the job of adjudicating (subject to appeal to the Supreme Court) on books and magazines referred to it. I have met its members and found them about as informed, sane and civilized a group as any country could produce. They expected abuse, braced themselves for it, and found it nearly all coming from book-banning zealots in the House of Representatives, with whom

1. Explained in The *Sunday Times* of 21st January, 1968.

they are now as popular as an ineffectual home goalkeeper.[1]

Publishers, anywhere, have no voice in the selection of the jurors who may one day read their books and condemn them for 'obscenity'. If jury trial and Lord Goodman's plan are seen as competing evils, Lord Goodman's plan is infinitely the lesser. He suggests also that a writer or publisher be given the chance to amend a manuscript and thus avoid prosecution, just as a theatre manager used to be 'consulted' by the Lord Chamberlain, and with the same scope for going defiantly ahead and taking what's coming. I have put this ingenious scheme under the 'impracticable' heading because (a) I believe the publishers would boycott it and (b) it might well confound its author's best intentions and grow into an instrument of oppression. But I may be wrong, and it has never been tried. Unlike the British Board of Film Censors, it would presumably be a statutory body, appointed by the authority of Parliament. It would take the place of today's haphazard relationship between the D.P.P. and a number of unknown psychiatrists, child experts, editors and writers. And if it were found to be growing tyrannical or – as some of its critics suggest – corrupt, a House of Commons that can rid the English theatre of the Lord Chamberlain would surely know what to do about one of its own experimental creatures.

THAT MULTIPLE BOOKSELLERS AND PUBLIC LIBRARIES SHOULD BE COMPELLED TO SUPPLY THE BOOKS THEY ARE ASKED FOR

This proposal concerns two forms of censorship that 'the reading public' finds particularly maddening. Here are examples of each. First, a letter, which is self-explanatory, sent by a friend of mine to the managing director of W. H. Smith & Sons Ltd. in London:

Dear Sir,

Publications not handled for sale

I recently had occasion to order through your North Finchley branch a copy of Sandford Friedman's novel *Totempole*, published in this country earlier this year by Anthony Blond. After some delay I was informed that it is

1. Their procedure is admirably explained in Stuart Perry's *The Indecent Publications Act*. Whitcombe and Tombs, 1966.

'not handled' by your firm. The reason given to me orally was that any book judged by your legal advisers to be at risk of a possible prosecution under the Obscene Publications Act is not sold.

So far as this particular book is concerned it has not only been the subject of favourable reviews in the responsible press but it is freely available in the local Public Library where it first came to my attention. Having thus read it on loan, I fear one would have to strain one's credulity to believe that so moving and perceptive a novel could ever be considered obscene – even by the irresponsible. I am, therefore, left with an uneasy feeling – bolstered by similar experiences of other members of the public – that your firm, contrary to the public interest, operates a private censorship of publications on subjects of which you do not approve and that this policy is camouflaged as commercial caution. Certainly, my inquiries reveal that, whereas reputable booksellers must naturally exercise their discretion in these matters, the policy adopted by your firm is of so arbitrary a nature as to be unprecedented in its application elsewhere.

I now write formally to request you to supply me with one copy of *Totempole* and on receipt of your agreement to do so I will send you my cheque for the required amount. If you decline to sell me this publication without good reason, I intend to have the matter ventilated in the Press.

In the meantime, I am sending a copy of this letter to Mr. Anthony Blond.

Yours faithfully,

A prompt and courteous reply came that W. H. Smith's had taken counsel's opinion on *Totempole* before deciding not to 'handle' it. They seemed undismayed at the prospect that my friend might 'ventilate the matter in the Press'. The Press, they said, was well aware of their decision about this book; and so was Mr. Anthony Blond.

My friend then wrote to me. What about this? he said. He saw me, I guessed, as the first step in the Press campaign. I knew nothing about *Totempole*, and still know nothing except that it has not been the subject of any prosecution in England and has not (so far as I know) been seized by customs officers, who operate their own little system. I wrote and told him, with the frankness possible among the best of friends, that

if I were a bookseller and he threatened me with Press
'exposure' because I didn't want to sell him any particular
book, I should tell him to go to hell. If enough people want
to buy books of a particular kind, the bookseller who won't
sell them will go under. I see nothing wrong with a Press
campaign against a 'censorship' operated by a bookseller.
He will always get space for an answer and he will never lack
supporters – the activists on both sides in this controversy
are highly literate people and they turn in good copy for the
correspondence pages, partly because they are perpetually
angry. But that's as far as I ever want to see the pressure go,
and even that has the dangers I have already pointed out.

Surely, said my friend, it isn't quite so simple? 'If I own
the largest chain of retail bookshops in the country, with a
virtual monopoly in many districts, would it be fair to the
public if I said: "Because I am a militant Roman Catholic
no books advocating unpermitted methods of birth control
will be sold in my shops"? Or "I don't mind making money
out of lurid sex paperbacks provided their setting is heterosexual, but I won't sell a serious novel on homosexuals as I
hate their guts"? To my mind', my friend concluded,
'people who think like that have no right to be booksellers.
To use power and near monopoly to deny people freedom of
choice under the law I find hard to stomach.'

'The right to be a bookseller' . . . But there is no more than
a right to survive as a bookseller if your customers want you
to survive the jungle war of supply and demand. 'To use
power and near-monopoly to deny people freedom of choice
. . .' This is a complaint about monopoly, and a valid one. A
huge multiple booksellers' business will never be in the
vanguard of adventurous bookselling, simply because it no
longer has any need to be. Its policy of 'censorship' is as
arbitrary as a man's choice of books for his own shelves at
home.

Next, a report from the *Manchester Guardian* of the 9th
July 1954:

JUDGMENT ON A BOOK DEFERRED.

Doubt About Censorship.

Caithness Library Sub-Committee yesterday deferred
judgment for another month on Bruce Marshall's novel

A Fair Bride, because all members had not read it. At last month's meeting of the committee, Mr. Owen R. Owen, of Wick, called it 'a most disgusting and most revolting book'.

Mr. Alec Miller, of Wick, said their system of censoring books did not appear to work well. 'When we bring a book up here it creates a prurient desire in people to read it – they think it is filthy. I am sure there was a big run on Boswell's *London Journal* after we had referred to it here.'

The county librarian said there was.

The multiple bookseller's policy is one that lays bare the special dangers of monopoly; and the library committee's is one that involves the admission of the press to local authorities' meetings. Neither can be improved by any plan to make them supply the books they are asked for. The reasons may be self-evident but they should be briefly stated here. First, 'compulsion' always necessitates a sanction of some kind. What do you do with a bookseller or librarian who says, 'I don't care what the law says about my obligations, that's not the kind of book we propose to handle'? Whatever coercion you can devise (and it usually has imprisonment at the far end of it), the final shape of it would enable the government to insist that booksellers sold and libraries lent whatever books the government thought the people should be reading.

THAT THE CUSTOMS AUTHORITIES SHOULD SEIZE ONLY THOSE OBSCENE ARTICLES ALREADY CONDEMNED IN BRITISH COURTS OF LAW

This is a favourite one with extreme libertarians and whole-hoggers. They contrive to forget that they want British courts of law to mind their own business anyway, and leave obscene books alone. I put it under the 'impracticables' because Great Britain has agreed, as a U.N. member, to co-operate with other countries in controlling the world trade in pornography. If this country was providing a good market for particularly outré kinds of French or German pornography, it would be no adequate answer to protests from the French or German government to say that there had not yet been a British prosecution concerning the stuff they wanted stopped at the ports.

THAT WHEN A TRAVELLER'S BOOK IS THUS SEQUESTERED, HE
SHOULD BE GIVEN A CHANCE TO READ IT, SO THAT HE CAN
CHALLENGE IN COURT THE CUSTOMS' DECISION

I wish this could come into the 'practicable' list; but I do
not see how the Customs men, if they think a book contra-
venes the International Convention, can allow its bearer to
take it away ostensibly to prepare its defence by reading it.
I do not see, either, why they should provide reading rooms
in which protesting book-importers could sit and read the
books they had innocently bought abroad. We all know that
the Customs men make mistakes, and I know a lot of funny
real life stories about them; but the stories do not advance
the matter at all, and I think we must leave the Customs men
to do their best, cursing them from time to time.

THAT THE POST OFFICE SHOULD BE DIVESTED OF ITS POWER TO
OPEN LETTERS IN SEARCH OF OBSCENITY

This is another favourite among freedom's champions. But
the Post Office, of its own initiative, has no such power. If
you complain to it that someone is mailing you unsolicited
obscenities, or if someone else informs it that this kind of
thing is going on, then it can open the indicated letters and
send anything 'obscene or indecent' that it finds to the
Director of Public Prosecutions. But of its own initiative it
can only open *unsealed* letters to see who is getting cheap
postage rates to which he is not entitled. True, there is a
prerogative power to intercept letters under a Home Office
warrant (and it will have to be made statutory when the
G.P.O. becomes a private enterprise and 'Royal Mail' comes
off all the vans); but oddly enough, this does not cover the
interception of obscenities.

All the foregoing proposals I would reject, in some cases
reluctantly, in others vehemently. It is a relief, therefore, to
turn now to those that seem to me practicable and desirable.

Practical Proposals

THAT 'BOOKS' BE EXEMPTED FROM THE OPERATION OF THE
OBSCENITY LAWS

This would necessitate a careful definition of 'books', in the
knowledge that anything not included would be controlled

by the law as to what one could safely publish. Hard-cover books? Books of not less than 40,000 words? Printed books, as distinct from lithographed, cyclostyled or photocopied manuscripts? But hard-cover books now form a diminishing proportion of the newly-published. You could never exclude paperbacks, some of which today cost more than many a hardback.

Would the 40,000 words have to be totally occupied by the theme of the book? If not, the most startling obscenity, running perhaps to not more than 5,000 words, could be padded out with 35,000 'lifted' from an out-of-copyright cookery book. There would be many difficulties of definition. I should like to see it attempted, for if it could be done I would be ready to see the censorship of 'books' abolished.

This is mainly because the law of England, for the older forms of which I have always had a profound respect, is made to look sadly ridiculous whenever a work of genuine literary achievement is prosecuted for obscenity; and the lawyers whose job it is to present such cases for the Crown, and whose phrases are taken up with unholy glee in the public prints by people like myself, are often and undeservedly labelled throughout their public life as silly and hypocritical Pecksniffs.

If we can satisfactorily define 'books', then let us stop burning them and punishing the men who produce them, and leave them to the laws of supply and demand and the vagaries of public taste. If that is too daring for current public acceptance, other proposals must be made; and they now follow:

THAT NO PRIVATE PERSON SHALL HAVE THE RIGHT TO PROSECUTE

It is necessary here to remember that, as a sequel to Sir Cyril Black's 'successful' action against *Last Exit to Brooklyn*, the private person has already lost his right to take out a summons for a 'destruction order'.[1] But he can still prosecute, which is something quite different. If you buy a book, borrow it from a library, or even read someone else's copy, and think it so obscene that its publishers ought to be

1. See p. 110.

punished, you can go to the Justice's Clerk's Office at the Magistrates' Court and say so. The Clerk will probably tell you to complain to the police; but I am supposing that you have either done so and been told to go away, or decided that you want to do the job yourself anyway. Before advising one of his magistrates to issue a summons against the publisher, the Clerk will want – or need – to read the book; and then the magistrate, if he is wise, will read it too and decide for himself. This will take longer than juries are allowed for their reading. It may take about a fortnight. (Neither the Magistrate nor his clerk would bother to read the book at this stage if the complaint came from the police or the Director of Public Prosecutions. But you might be a crank.) Then the publisher will receive a summons saying, on the strength of your information,[1] that he is accused of publishing 'an obscene article' and that he is to attend before the Magistrates on a given date – perhaps about another fortnight off. On that day you can go to court and either present the case yourself or instruct a solicitor to do it for you. (You will have to pay him.)

The Magistrate, who will have read the book, will nevertheless hear what you have to say; and you may find that the publisher is calling a lot of witnesses to swear that, whether or not the book is what the law calls obscene, it is of such literary, artistic or other excellence that the public ought to have it if they want it. You can bring your own witnesses to swear otherwise. You may have to pay their expenses, fares and loss of earnings; and if you lose your case, you almost certainly will. The Magistrate may decide that the case ought to be tried by a jury; and if he does, neither you nor the publisher can stop it. There will be a delay of some weeks, possibly two or three months; and you will now find that you must either engage a barrister (as well as the solicitor you are already paying) or relinquish the whole conduct of the case and let the Director of Public Prosecutions take it over.

He may step in and take it over anyway; and if he does, it is quite possible that having got rid of you he will 'offer no

1. And *not* as a result of the Magistrate and his clerk having read the book.

evidence' and ask for the case to be dismissed. (The book itself will not be sufficient evidence – there has to be proof that the defendant published it, and when and where.)

How important, then, is this private right to prosecute publishers? When the sponsors of the Obscene Publications Act were trying to get the D.P.P. made officially responsible for every case, there was strong opposition from some right-wing lawyers in both Houses. They spoke of the private citizen's 'right to prosecute' as one of the great traditional liberties. And they won, though a study of the Parliamentary debates suggests that this, so far from being a victory for constitutional rights, was a triumph for the Law Officers who didn't want any extra work.

It would do no violence to the civil liberties to take away this notional right. It has been taken away in respect of many crimes and it never existed in others (e.g., the Official Secrets Act). Any future Statute on the subject of 'obscene publications' should abolish the 'rights' of private prosecutors, which are now no more consonant with social needs or legal practice than were those of that unsavoury survival, the common informer.[1]

THAT THE 'CRIME' OF PUBLISHING AN OBSCENE ARTICLE SHOULD BE ABOLISHED, AND THAT ANY PROCEEDINGS SHOULD BE FOR FORFEITURE ONLY

The purpose of inflicting punishment on the *person* of the publisher, or making him pay a fine as well as losing his books, can only now be vengeful and (perhaps optimistically) deterrent to others. It is an anachronism. Prison is not the place – whoever else may be justifiably there – for someone who has done no more than publish a book. The fitness of a fine, on the other hand, depends on the number of books seized by the police and now to be burned or pulped by order of the court – a number that may be three or 3,000. However many copies are destroyed by order of the court, he would be a bold publisher who decided to go ahead, and sell the rest of the copies in stock. After the decision that *Fanny Hill* must be destroyed, the publisher wrote to all the retailers

1. He was abolished by Statute in 1951.

who might still have copies in stock and offered them their money back if they returned the goods. None came back. Under-the-counter sales were too brisk. But the situation would have been no different if there had been a prosecution and a conviction, followed by a destruction order. Prosecution and punishment, in fact, achieves nothing beyond the infliction of some kind of suffering. Probably the forfeiture proceedings would satisfy most of the moralists and the punishers if the consequences could be made plain to all. The people still dissatisfied would be in respectable company, for the love of punishment (for others) is deeply ingrained in decent society.

THAT (IF THE ABOVE IS UNACCEPTABLE) THE DEFENDANT AND NOT THE D.P.P. SHOULD ELECT THE MODE OF TRIAL

As was noted at the beginning of Chapter VI, the behaviour of the authorities in deciding whether to prosecute or merely to ask for forfeiture has been noticeably lacking in any kind of pattern; and the decisions have often (and fruitlessly) been challenged at Question Time in the House of Commons.

Studying the cases, it is impossible to resist the conclusion that the paramount consideration is not justice but administrative convenience. Whatever happens about the mass production and sale of 'pin-up' magazines etc., whose representatives never want to go before juries,[1] the publishers of anything you could reasonably call a book should be given the choice of forfeiture proceedings or trial by jury on criminal proceedings. It should not be the choice of the D.P.P.

THAT THERE SHOULD BE A RIGHT OF TRIAL BY JURY IN FORFEITURE PROCEEDINGS AS WELL AS IN CRIMINAL PROSECUTIONS

The right to jury trial in the criminal proceedings is inviolate. The 1959 Act confers it and no House of Commons would ever allow it to be taken away. Why has it always been withheld in forfeiture proceedings?

---

1. At Brighton Borough Sessions on 1st November, 1963, one of these received the staggering sentence of five years' imprisonment (*R.* v. *Oswin*, 1964).

The difficulty is one of precedent and jurisdiction. To confer such a right would be to require a jury in an exclusively criminal court to decide something which is a 'civil' issue: civil rather than criminal because no punishment, as such, can be imposed on the defendant. He merely loses his book or books – and perhaps pays heavy costs. This is not called punishment, though no doubt many a publisher or bookseller has searched in vain for the difference.

But the difficulty is a notional one merely. Criminal juries in the past have often been required to try non-criminal matters. A quaint example was the Sentence of Death (Expectant Mothers) Act, 1931, now repealed. The law would not allow, in death penalty days, the execution of a pregnant woman. This Act required that when a woman stood convicted of murder, and it was pleaded on her behalf that she was 'quick with child', a 'jury of matrons' (i.e., married women) must be empanelled to hear medical evidence and decide upon her condition. What other decision they could have come to, after hearing doctors say that she was quick with child, was never revealed. But the decision required of them was not a criminal verdict.

In the debates on the Obscene Publications Bill 1964, Mr. Neill MacDermot, Q.C. (later Solicitor-General) made a threefold suggestion about this:

1. Abolish the forfeiture procedure altogether and make forfeiture an 'ancillary order' following conviction; or

2. Allow trial by jury in forfeiture cases, which 'would mean a considerable administrative change in the law'; or

3. If a serious defence of literary merit is claimed as soon as the police begin their enquiries, then proceedings should be by prosecution, never by forfeiture.

But the then Solicitor-General, Sir Peter Rawlinson, Q.C., was more hopeful:

There is certainly no objection in principle [he said] to proceedings for forfeiture being tried by jury in courts of criminal jurisdiction. It would be an innovation but that should not prevent it happening. There *are* problems, and there should be considerable hesitation before this procedure is introduced.

So the idea 'would be studied', he concluded. The study produced no effect whatever on the 1964 Bill, but filed away somewhere in the Home Office there must be some memoranda on its pros and cons. I should be surprised if the pros were not the stronger.

THAT THERE SHOULD BE A TIME LIMIT BETWEEN SEIZURE AND HEARING

If the forfeiture proceedings are to be retained, the police should not need more than 14 days in which to make up their minds about the books they have been reading. They presumably had some idea of their obscenity before seizing them at all, and undue delay inflicts needless anxiety.

The procedure at present is that the police buy or in some way acquire copies of the publications they want to get destroyed. They take them to a magistrate. If he thinks them obscene, he issues a search warrant to seize any more like them in the same premises. That search and seizure must be carried out within 14 days[1]; otherwise it will be unlawful and actionable. But there is no time limit, thereafter, within which the police must apply for 'the summons to show cause' why the books should not be forfeited and destroyed.

There have been cases in which four, five and six months have gone by, and in 1951 there was in one case a delay of nine months – which, said the High Court, made no difference to the validity of the destruction order. But Lord Devlin remarked: 'I should not like it to be thought that it is open to the police to take any amount of time they want, merely because there is no statutory time limit.'

The magistrate who issued the search warrant (or, more probably, his clerk) can keep the police on their toes if he is so minded. After about a fortnight he could ask them when he could expect to see the fruits of his warrant. Or he could issue his summons without waiting for them. It might be a good idea to make this mandatory after one month if the police have not acted earlier.

1. Obscene Publications Act, 1959, Section 3 (1).

THAT THE JURY SHOULD BE EFFECTIVELY REQUIRED TO READ THE BOOK

'Take the book home, members of the jury,' said Mr. Justice Stable in *The Philanderer* case, 'and read it by yourselves: don't talk about it to anybody.'

'The average rate of reading is, I think, 298 words a minute,' said Mr. Gerald Gardiner in the *Chatterley* case. 'Which is rather less than a page. On that footing this book will take the average reader between seven and eight hours. . . . Those hours they will have to spend reading cheek by jowl, which no one who bought it would do. It would save any possibility of the jury being embarrassed if they were allowed to read it at home.'

'I think the jury should read the book here,' said Mr. Justice Byrne. 'I'm very sorry, members of the jury, but if you were to take this book home, you might have distractions . . . I think it would be much better if you were to read this book in your room.'

His Lordship had said that he remembered within his own experience juries reading prosecuted books in the jury room. Many people in Court, on the other hand, remembered juries taking the books home. There seems to be no pattern, either in the place of reading or the time allowed. Some members of the jury that tried *Last Exit to Brooklyn* said they had finished it in 'a little over an hour'. Only one took more than five hours. The publishers, Calder & Boyars, said in a letter to *The Times* on the 2nd December 1967 that:

> most persons who have read it for review or to help the defence took considerably longer than five hours, and they are highly literate people.

The publishers thought some of the jury simply hadn't read the book, and it may even have been that some of them couldn't.

The jury that tried *Lady Chatterley's Lover*, and were not allowed to take it home, took three days over it.

How do you discover whether all the jurors have read the book? It is simply impossible, most lawyers seem to say. I suggest that a simple questionnaire, based on the theme and message of the book and agreed by both Counsel with the

Judge, could be prepared for the jurors to answer in isolation; and that to allow for failures the number sworn should be fifteen instead of twelve. (Fifteen are commonly empanelled to try felony cases in Californian courts, the three 'extras' sitting by the side of the jury-box in case they are needed.) All the time this is said to be impracticable it will never be done, and no obscenity trial by jury will ever be just. The jurors should in general take the book home to read, but any juror who preferred to read it in the Court precincts should be allowed to do so.

The questionnaire would incidentally discover which of the jurors were able to read at all.

THE CHARGE OF 'CONSPIRING' TO CONTRAVENE THE ACT SHOULD BE ABOLISHED

It has been well established since the late seventeenth century that a conspiracy to commit any crime 'or other wrong' is itself a crime.[1] An indictment for Common Law conspiracy is an ingenious trap for almost any defendant, since it lets in evidence not admissible on a substantive charge and plays off one defendant against another. The sponsors of the Obscene Publications Bill tried to get rid of the Common Law indictment altogether. This, instead, is what they had got when the Bill was through:

> A person publishing an article shall not be proceeded against for an offence at common law consisting of the publication of any matter contained or embodied in the article, where it is of the essence of the offence that the matter is obscene.

No one seems to know what it means, but anyone who supposed that it meant the end of Common Law indictments for obscenity was quickly disillusioned. It is generally taken to mean that a prosecution for *publishing* an obscenity must now be under the 1959 Act and not under the Common Law. But this has not hitherto prevented Common Law prosecutions for *conspiring* to publish obscenities in breach of the Act; and the advantage of these to the prosecution is that probably

---

1. Holdsworth, *History of English Law*, VIII, 302.

they will rule out the possibility of calling evidence about 'public good' and 'literary merit'.[1]

When the 1964 Bill was under debate in the Commons Mr. Roy Jenkins tried to get this clarified:

The Bill should include a provision stating that if the prosecuting authorities wish to take conspiracy proceedings, then there should be an explicit declaration, in a statutory form, that all the safeguards of the 1959 Act will be applied.

But conspiracy prosecutions have continued unabated.

THAT ALL LOCAL ACTS AND BY-LAWS IN CONFLICT WITH THE INTENTION OF THE OBSCENE PUBLICATIONS ACT SHOULD BE REPEALED

There is an immense list of these and they are to be found in a great variety of cities, towns and counties throughout Great Britain. They range from 'public general' Acts of Parliament like the Vagrancy Act of 1824 (with its three months' imprisonment for 'exhibiting obscene prints', etc.) to a 1961 Edinburgh Corporation By-law of similar effect. They all facilitate summary prosecutions that permit no expert evidence in defence; they do not reach the notice of the Director of Public Prosecutions; and they expose the publisher to local hazards over which Parliament has either lost or has abdicated all control. The original 1959 Bill was so drafted as to get rid of all these local gadflies but its sponsors were told, by the Home Office legal men and the Parliamentary Bills Office, that a Private Member's Bill cannot be used for that purpose. When it appeared, the Government's own Bill seemed to suffer from the same inhibition, for the gadflies all survived.

Their repeal or revocation is one of the most urgent reforms in the whole field of 'censorship'.

THE 'TWO-STAGE' TRIAL

I come last of all to a proposition of my own. It can be valid only so long as the law maintains its present attitude to book

1. Not all lawyers are agreed that this is so, but they never seem to put it to the test.

publishing, and I take this opportunity to repeat the hope that a way will be found to exempt books altogether. Until then, we should face the somewhat tortuous logic of the present Statute and try to make it work better.

It is a paradox, the product of mixed intentions of a wholly beneficent character, that a book can be found to be both obscene and good for the public. Remember that to be obscene it must have a 'tendency to deprave and corrupt'.[1] The Statute says (in effect) that although a book is obscene in that sense it will be above the law

> if it is proved (by experts) that publication of the article in question is justified as being for the public good, on the grounds that it is in the interests of science, literature, art or learning, or of other objects of general concern.

'If it is proved' merely means if a particular jury can be induced to believe it. Lest it be supposed that this provision in the Act of 1959 reflects some peculiarly asinine English compromise, it should be mentioned that roughly similar provisions existed before 1959 (and still exist) in the law of New South Wales, Queensland, Tasmania, Victoria, Western Australia, Canada, New Zealand, India and Pakistan (where the idols and temples are specially singled out for exemption), Belgium, Western Germany, Switzerland and the U.S.S.R. In France, Sweden and Japan literary or artistic excellence is no defence though it may provide mitigation.

In some countries the 'public good' question is (as in England) a matter of fact for the jury to decide: in others it is a matter of law for the judge to decide.

It seems to me that all the time this apparent contradiction exists, judges and juries alike will be in the difficult position, despite the new 'guidance' given by the Court of Appeal in the *Last Exit* case, of men trying to reconcile the irreconcilable. The solution I offer is that there should be two separate trials. The jury having read the book, having heard only the kind of proceedings they could have heard before 1959, namely the details about the purchase of the book, the date and place of its publication, and the defendant's good

1. For the meanings of these two words see page 18.

reputation, and then the speeches of Counsel and the Judge's summing up on the question of obscenity, will return their verd ct *on that question alone*. If they say 'Not Guilty', that is absolutely final. Up to that stage, no 'expert witnesses' are engaged. No one, therefore, has been waiting expensively around to give evidence for the defence. The case is over, everyone goes home, and the defendant may have saved himself thousands of pounds.

But if the jury says 'Guilty', then the question of public good and literary merit arises for the first time. If the defendant wants to avail himself of it, then – and only then – a second trial takes place; not immediately, but a week later, and with the same jury. The defendant's solicitors have had all the necessary letters ready to send off (if need be) to the chosen witnesses, the literary dons, the poets, the professors of moral theology, the critics. At the end of the second trial the jury must decide whether the book, though obscene, is one that ought to be published, like the *Satyricon* of Petronius, the *Satires* of Juvenal, the *Kama Sutra* – and *Last Exit to Brooklyn*.

There are precedents in English law for such a two-stage trial. There was, for example, the Sentence of Death (Expectant Mothers) Act, 1931, which directed that when a jury had found a woman guilty of murder and she was said to be pregnant, there should be a second trial to decide whether she was.[1] There was, in the Prevention of Crimes Act, 1908, a provision for two separate trials in the process of sending a 'habitual criminal' to 'preventive detention'. First, the jury tried him on the charge for which he had been arrested – burglary, false pretences, robbery, etc. If they said 'Not Guilty', that was the end of it. If they said 'Guilty', a second trial took place at once, with the same jury, to decide whether the prisoner came within the statutory meaning of the phrase 'habitual criminal'; in which event he could get, in addition to his sentence for the burglary, a period of preventive detention of anything from 8 to 15 years. They heard evidence (a) that he was over 30 and under 70, (b) that three times since the age of 16 he had been convicted of grave crime, and (c) that he was at present 'obtaining his livelihood

1. See also p. 132.

by dishonest means'. The first two points were proved easily from the records, and gave a jury no scope. The third was the issue on which many a man thus tried was acquitted: juries being often unconvinced that he was getting his living dishonestly – they saw the crime they had just convicted him of as a momentary lapse or 'a cry for help'. So sometimes he got merely the sentence due to him for the burglary. Once or twice I have seen such a man put on probation, even though the jury found that he *was* a habitual criminal; the long prison sentence was never mandatory. The procedure, and the phrase 'habitual criminal', were abolished in 1948 by a Criminal Justice Act which nevertheless continued preventive detention and made it rather easier to get. In 1967 it was finally abolished by the good old English legislative process of calling it something else. (It is now an 'extended sentence'.)

On the civil side, it is now proposed by Lord Justice Winn's Committee on 'Personal Injuries Litigation' that there should be 'split trials' to decide liability and damages separately. The legal precedents that would support the two-trial proposal seem, accordingly, respectable enough.

VII

A WORD
IN YOUR EAR

So much for the law and what might be done (if it can't be abolished) to improve it. I want to end with two or three questions: always the easiest way to end, because questions can be made to look impressive while in fact they conceal a hopelessly equivocal state of mind. These questions have to do with the assault of the anti-reticence enthusiasts upon our privacy.

Are the various forms of mass communication combining now to annihilate our personal integrity? Privacy is the part of the human condition that has taken the longest to grow: the process must have begun, in a very small way, soon after we came down from the trees. Apes built, and build, no lavatories. There could have been little privacy in the forest clearings where the early Britons slept, loved and scratched. By Victoria's time, privacy was a civil right as inalienable as a decent funeral; even the very poor contrived to get as much as they could. It may have been a selfish and anti-social aim. It had two watchwords: 'Am I my brother's keeper?'[1] and the oft-misquoted 'The house of everyone is to him as his castle and fortress.'[2] We slammed our front doors and we were in private. No telephone, no television or radio, no delivered newspapers, not even – in many front doors – a letter-box.

It could hardly last, and perhaps it was right that it shouldn't. But it was the apex of the privacy graph; if there was to be a change it could only be downwards, less privacy

1. Genesis, IV, 9.
2. Sir Edward Coke, in *Semayne's Case Reports*, Vol. 5, p. 91 b.

and less, down towards the long-lost status of the ape; but taking with us our books, newspapers, films, plays and television. Too much has been written about all this and there is much more to come. I content myself with a simple image, to illustrate our expanding condition of zoological frankness. When lovers exchange their first abandoned kiss, they still tend to do it in private. When the occasion comes in a television play, and it is being done for the entertainment of an assembled family, the people kissing often present the appearance of two people trying to swallow the same oyster. The assembled family sits it through because to do anything else would seem ridiculous. But a miniature brick has been pulled away from the huge and precarious edifice of personal dignity, and the value of privacy has fallen microscopically.

We all know where we're going, and what we are forsaking. About ten years ago *The Times* published a valedictory leader about what we were forsaking. It was headed 'A Certain Reticence'. It caused untold merriment, most of the other papers being convulsed with glee. Oh, it was funny, *The Times*. Much has happened to our privacy since then, and the assault continues.

INDEX